The Healing Energy of Shared Consciousness

A Taoist Approach to Entering the Universal Mind

Mantak Chia

Destiny Books
Rochester, Vermont • Toronto, Canada

Destiny Books
One Park Street
Rochester, Vermont 05767
www.DestinyBooks.com

Destiny Books is a division of Inner Traditions International

Originally published in Thailand in 2008 by Universal Tao Publications under the title *Universal World Link: Healing Yourself and Others through the Cosmos*

Library of Congress Cataloging-in-Publication Data
Chia, Mantak, 1944–
  [Universal world link]
  The healing energy of shared consciousness : a Taoist approach to entering the universal mind / Mantak Chia.
       p. cm.
  Originally published: Universal world link. Thailand : Universal Tao Publications, 2008.
  Includes index.
  ISBN 978-1-59477-321-1 (pbk.)
  1. Taoism—Miscellanea. I. Title.

BL1923.C45 2011
299.5'14435—dc22
                                                              2010037713
Printed and bound in India by Replika Press Pvt. Ltd.

10 9 8 7 6 5 4 3 2 1

Text design and layout by Priscilla Baker
This book was typeset in Janson, with Sho, Present, and Futura used as display typefaces

 Contents

Acknowledgments

The Universal Tao Publications staff involved in the preparation and production of this book extend our gratitude to the many generations of Taoist Masters who have passed on their special lineage, in the form of an unbroken oral transmission, over thousands of years. We thank Taoist Master Yi Eng for his openness in transmitting the formulas of Taoist Inner Alchemy. We also wish to thank the thousands of unknown men and women of the Chinese healing arts who developed many of the methods and ideas presented in this book.

We offer our eternal gratitude and love to our parents and teachers for their many gifts to us. Remembering them brings joy and satisfaction to our continued efforts in presenting the Universal Tao System. As always, their contribution has been crucial in presenting the concepts and techniques of the Universal Tao.

We thank the many contributors essential to this book's final form: Juan Li for the use of his beautiful and visionary paintings and drawings, illustrating Taoist esoteric practices, the editorial and production staff at Inner Traditions/Destiny Books for their efforts to clarify the text and produce a handsome new edition of the book, and Patty Capetola for her line edit of the new edition.

We wish to thank the following people for their assistance in producing the original edition of this book: Lee Holden for his writing contributions, Matthew Koren for his editorial work, Suthisa Chaisarn for his design and production work, and W. U. Wei for his production management.

A special thanks goes to our Thai production team: Raruen Keawapadung, computer graphics; Saysunee Yongyod, photographer; Udon Jandee, illustrator; and Saniem Chaisarn, production designer.

# Introduction

My wish is for every person to be spiritually independent and to connect directly to the source, cosmos, primordial force, or creative force in our common quest for return to the Wu Chi (God). Through this process, we can gain inner peace and happiness. We can also gain the ability to heal ourselves and others, too. Naturally, the first step is to be at peace and to be happy with ourselves as we work to accomplish our goals. Therefore, I have devised this meditation practice, the World Link of Protective Healing, which becomes especially profound when the effect of its healing energy is amplified by many others in a circle of shared consciousness and awareness. In preparation for the World Link of Protective Healing, we always employ the use of the Protective Sacred Circle of Fire, which creates a protective seal that allows only good energy and intentions in. Negative energy cannot penetrate the circle. Once we are prepared, we look within to heal our own hearts, invoking different energies to purify and restore us, before we finally work on sending positive, healing energy out into the world.

The universe has an abundance of energy that can enhance and multiply our enjoyment of life. All that we need to do is to be connected to the source. Through this powerful meditation practice, we manifest the energy that resides in our three minds. The first mind is the observing mind, which is centered in the brain. The second is called the conscious mind, and it is centered in the heart. The third is the mind of awareness, and is centered in the lower abdomen, that is, the abdominal brain. The three minds combine to fuse together in the abdomen, creating one mind. In Chinese, this one mind is called Yi (pronounced ee). By encountering the world with a unified mind, we can create and transform the energy that is directed at us into positive energy. This can result in a more balanced, less negative energy for our culture and the institutions created to serve us.

The World Link of Protective Healing meditation practice is designed to move your awareness from operating primarily in your upper mind to more actively using your middle and lower minds as well. By moving your focus to different areas of your being, you will begin to uncover new aspects of your being, some of which you may not have been aware before. This causes an opening or space that allows for a new reality to exist. Ultimately, this will empower you to effect positive change not only in yourself but in your greater world. By accessing this new space, you allow your goals and dreams to become manifest in your life. Once your energy becomes focused from a place of power and love, you can send that loving energy out to benefit the world and the surrounding universe.

"Where your mind goes, the Chi follows." By moving your awareness from your upper mind down to the lower two minds, the energy will follow. This will activate your middle and lower minds, enabling you to recognize and process the information from those nerve centers. By practicing this formula, you'll begin to do this automatically.

The ideal outcome is that you will learn how to feel with your mind and think with your heart. Think what would happen if the whole world began to do this. The outcome would be peace and harmony, the end of conflict and war. This can happen one person at a time or in a group of people. This formula is designed to be practiced with multiple people at similar times across the world. Hopefully, by reading and sharing this formula with others, you can begin to develop a network of people dedicating the immense power of their minds to the benefit of everyone on this earth.

Through this powerful healing meditation practice, practitioners gain access to a method to move energy, both the energy around them and that in their environment, and then to focus it for good intentions and positive transformation. When people from all around the world link together at the same time, they are greatly empowered. The

World Link of Protective Healing can be practiced easily, even by those who have never worked with the Universal Tao practices.

It is my hope that by disseminating this method, I might encourage people to develop a regular practice for manifesting not only what they would like to see happen in their own lives, but also to manifest energy in such a way that the world itself benefits from their positive intentions. A single meditator can effect tremendous change in his or her own life through regular and focused practice. Imagine a group of meditators practicing together with similar intentions for themselves and their world! What joy they can bring!

Link Time: Thailand 12:00 Noon; New York 12:00 Midnight; Europe 6:00 in the morning. Find your time zone; it could be one hour before or after these morning and evening times.

The World Link of Protective Healing is a spiritual practice that takes around 15 to 30 minutes. As stated, this powerful series of meditations is designed to focus and purify the mind so that positive energy can be projected out into the world by its practitioners. The practice starts with an explanation of the concepts behind each stage of the practice, so that each practitioner may intentionally and powerfully engage in the meditations. The preparation consists of three parts: first, a centering exercise; second, the Activation of the Consciousness of the Three Fires; and third, the creation of the Sacred Circle of Fire. Afterward, the practitioner is prepared to begin moving energy around to intentionally heal himself or herself physically, emotionally, and spiritually. By healing oneself, one heals the world.

With the simple practice of the Inner Smile, in which we smile down to all our internal organs, we can integrate our bodies, minds, and spirits.* They become no longer separate. The World Link

---

*For more specific directions on how to practice the basic Inner Smile meditation, see my book *The Inner Smile* (Rochester, Vt.: Destiny Books, 2008).

Meditation expands on this exercise by going into more depth about the dynamics of the Inner Smile. The strength of the three minds is revealed when each of the faculties of observation, consciousness, and awareness are combined and connected with the forces of the six directions (i.e., above, below, left, right, front, and back), drawing and fusing a sublimation of all of these external energies into the body. Eventually, with practice, one can draw upon many different energies and use them as needed, thereby giving form to the formless energy that is abundant in the universe.

THREE TAN TIENS

In Taoist practice, we think of our mind as being composed of three major nerve centers in the human body, all of which we use to encounter the world. The upper tan tien is located within the upper brain, the middle tan tien is located in the heart, and the lower tan tien is in the abdomen. These three minds correspond to the three tan tiens, or major energy centers, within the body. They can store, transform, and supply energy to and from each other, as well as the spinal cord, the sexual organs, and other major organs. All the tan tiens have both yin and yang within them. In nature, the yin and yang are present in all things.

The upper tan tien is located in the upper brain (the Crystal Palace). When it is full of energy, the brain functions with an increased capacity. The upper mind is associated with observation. It subjectively projects positive and negative energy at every moment. Using only a limited range of information, which it gathers from observing its surroundings, the upper mind likes to come to a conclusion or judgment about the state of your world. In this processing, the upper mind uses about 80 percent of your energy. This is too much!

Of course, we need the upper mind to focus on particular stimuli in our environment, but if it starts to think and make decisions, we are very often led astray. This is because the upper mind, by its natural way of processing, doesn't use all of the information available. Its job is to ignore most of the information in your environment so that you can focus and observe from one perspective. But observations are not answers to your questions, and one perspective is not the only way to view any particular topic. As human beings, we need to use our other minds to come up with the answers to questions that we ask ourselves. The Taoist turns the self inward to the universe within, the microcosmic reflection of the macrocosm without.

The heart center, located between the two nipples, is the location of the middle tan tien. The middle mind is regarded as the seat of consciousness. Associated with fire and thought to be the site of original spirit (*shen*), the heart is the center of positive yang energy and is the gateway for manifesting healing energy throughout the body. It is associated with the virtuous emotions of love, respect, compassion, joy, and happiness. It is also associated with the thymus gland, which produces white blood cells, combating disease in the body.

The abdominal region surrounding the navel is like an empty universe or a vast ocean. It is regarded as the lower tan tien. It contains the lower mind and is associated with feeling and awareness. Within this universe or ocean, there is a fire, like a volcano under the ocean: "fire under water." Thus the three tan tiens refer to the three reservoirs and sources of energy within the body.

While resting, we should train our upper mind to simply observe. Any excess energy should be lowered through the middle tan tien to the lower tan tien and stored there (fig. I.1).

By lowering the excess energy in the upper mind to the lower mind, you can use the lower mind to do your thinking. By combining the three minds into one, you can use minimum effort to achieve maximum effect.

The heart resides in a special position where it connects the relationship of the upper and lower mind. This becomes manifest in our everyday experience when we are establishing a connection with our friends and loved ones. First, one might appeal to her gut reaction to judge another person. This is the feeling she gets just from interacting with someone for a short time. However, she might allow her upper

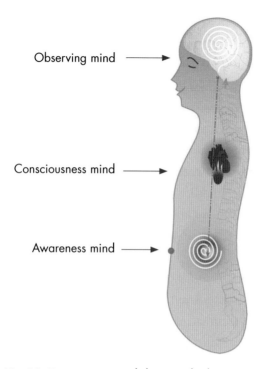

Observing mind

Consciousness mind

Awareness mind

Fig. I.1. Empty your mind down to the lower tan tien. Let awareness and consciousness combine together.

mind to evaluate and judge the other person first. After a period of time in the other person's presence, she will have had ample information coming from both the upper and lower mind. As this information travels back and forth, it crosses through the heart center. The heart processes and synthesizes all this information with its emotional record of the body when interacting with this person. All this information is coalesced and synthesized in the heart and projected to the other in an emotional connection with the other person's heart. It is rare that a person would immediately establish a heart connection with another human being unless a connection had already been present on some level.

The information from the upper and lower minds serves as a frame in which all our emotions are stored. This is why the love connections created in the heart are so strong. When someone falls in love with another person, they have no doubt experienced lots of pleasurable emotions, which begin to fill into the upper and lower minds' structure. These connections are extremely hard to break because all the emotions we've ever felt toward that person are encapsulated in this connection. These all are released when the upper or lower mind begins to change, or worse, sever the connection.

At first, I did not understand this. When my master taught me to lower and sink my mind down to the lower tan tien, I started to understand. Later, I understood this further, when I found that Western technology had discovered that the nerve endings in the stomach and intestines, especially those related to emotional responses, are the same as those in the upper mind. So by just smiling to the lower tan tien, you can activate the lower mind. By using the aware, conscious, and observing minds together in the abdomen, you can do all your thinking.

The upper mind works practically all the time, stirring up the emotions and using up your body's energy. Western science has discovered that the lower mind can do a lot of things that the upper mind does without using the senses. It does it with pure awareness, without questioning. Medical science refers to the lower mind as the enteric nervous system, responsible from the dawn of human existence for digesting and managing the chemical balance in the esophagus, stomach, small intestine, and colon. Indeed, many of the chemicals in the human brain are also found in the gut. Through emerging fields such as neurogastroenterology, modern scientists continue to examine how the upper and lower minds are connected.

If you can use the lower brain more, the upper mind can rest and listen (observe) from the abdomen. The upper mind, or as the Taoists refer to it, the monkey mind, when activated, will suppress consciousness or awareness. Once the upper mind rests, you can be conscious and aware of things of which you were never conscious or aware before. As you save energy by using the lower brain, your upper brain can rest and build up strength to cope with any daily stress.

Preparatory World Link Practices

The following series of exercises will prepare the individual or group to both project healing energy to the heart of the universe and to receive the healing energy from the universe. Here you will learn how to fuse the three minds into one mind (Yi), how to become aware of your personal star, expand the consciousness of your personal star out into the universe, join your personal star to the stars of others in your group, and finally, create an energy body that links everyone with the heart of the universe in unconditional love.

In preparation, we will center ourselves, fuse the energies of our three tan tiens, and finally create a Protective and Sacred Circle of Fire. In so doing, we will repel negative energy and ensure the creation of positive energy as we go forth.

Centering Meditation

1. Stand or sit alone or with others in a group meditation.
2. Relax and empty your mind down to the lower tan tien by smiling down to your lower abdomen (fig. 1.1).
3. Bring your awareness to your abdomen and fill your abdominal brain with chi.

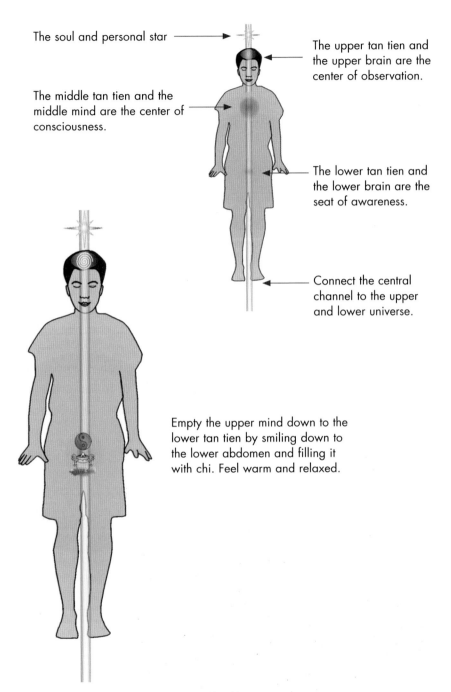

The soul and personal star

The upper tan tien and the upper brain are the center of observation.

The middle tan tien and the middle mind are the center of consciousness.

The lower tan tien and the lower brain are the seat of awareness.

Connect the central channel to the upper and lower universe.

Empty the upper mind down to the lower tan tien by smiling down to the lower abdomen and filling it with chi. Feel warm and relaxed.

Fig. 1.1. The three tan tiens

Activate the Consciousness of the Three Fires in the Tan Tien, Kidneys, and Heart

Tan Tien Fire (Abdomen)

1. Feel the energy behind the navel become warm as you direct a golden sunshine smile down from your eyes.
2. Imagine that the energy in your abdomen is like a fireball behind the navel and sits above a stove burning with fire (fig. 1.2). The stove is situated below the navel and close to the sacrum and lumbar vertebrae. Create the fireball above the stove behind the navel. The Taoists describe this as a burning stove that energizes the other fires in the body.

Smile down to the abdomen to create a burning stove near the lower lumbar and sacrum. Create a fireball behind the navel above the stove.

Fig. 1.2. Activating the tan tien fire

❧ *Fire under the Sea (Kidney)*

1. Be aware of the yang energy of the adrenals on top of the kidneys (fig. 1.3).
2. Move that yang energy down into the center of each kidney at the Door of Life (yang within the yin), thus lighting the Fire under the Sea.
3. Expand the activated kidney energy to the Door of Life point on the spine opposite the navel, just below the kidneys.

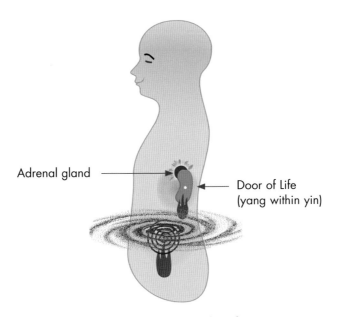

Fig. 1.3. Activating the kidney fire

❧ *Imperial Fire (Heart)*

1. Activate the consciousness by smiling down to the heart, making it feel soft.
2. Be aware of the fire in the heart (see fig. 1.4 on page 12). Feel the fire of love, joy, happiness, and compassion creating softness in the heart (yin within the yang), activating the heart's consciousness.
3. Make a triangle, connecting the heart down to the kidneys and then down to the tan tien fireball behind the navel. Connect the

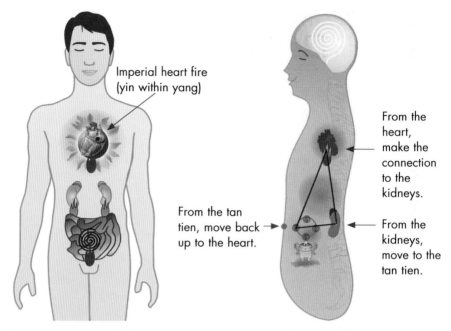

Imperial heart fire
(yin within yang)

From the tan
tien, move back
up to the heart.

From the
heart,
make the
connection
to the
kidneys.

From the
kidneys,
move to the
tan tien.

Fig. 1.4. Activating the heart fire

Fig. 1.5. The triple force is the Sacred Fire. Make a triangle connecting heart, kidneys, and tan tien.

fireball to the kidneys and back to the heart (fig. 1.5). This triangulation doubles or triples the chi fire power.

☸ Fuse the Three Minds into One Mind (Yi)

When the abdomen is filled with chi and feels warm and nice, it will rise and fill the upper brain with chi.

○ Smile to the Inner Universe

1. Place your palms together in salutation, in front of your heart (1.6a). Feel the Laogong points at the center of your palms connect (fig. 1.7), creating an energy loop running from your heart through your arms and hands and back again. Lower the middle mind to the lower tan tien (fig. 1.6a).

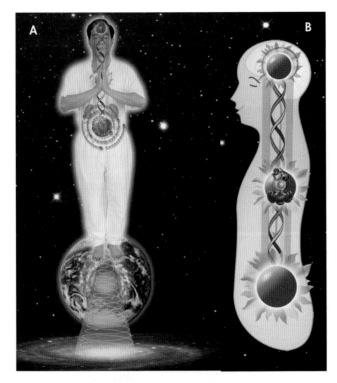

Fig. 1.6. A. Empty the mind
down to the lower abdomen.
B. Activate the heart's compassion.

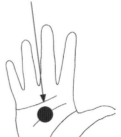

Laogong point
(Pericardium 8)

Fig. 1.7. The Laogong
point at the center of
the palm

O Activate the Heart Compassion Energy

1. Smile to the heart and feel it softening. Feel love, joy, compassion, and happiness.
2. Smiling down, lower the middle mind to the lower tan tien as you empty the mind to the abdominal brain.
3. Fill the third tan tien with chi and start to spiral (1.6b). When the abdomen is warm, it is full of chi. The chi can then charge up the brain.

⭕ Combine the Three Minds into One

1. Turn the upper mind into an observation mind.
2. Turn consciousness, the middle mind, down to the lower tan tien.
3. Focusing on the lower tan tien, combine the three minds into one mind, called Yi.
4. Let the Yi energy rise to the area behind your third eye (fig. 1.8). You can use this unified mind to make better decisions and to take correct action.

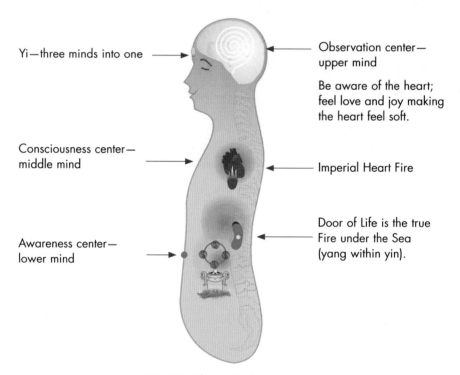

Yi—three minds into one

Observation center— upper mind

Be aware of the heart; feel love and joy making the heart feel soft.

Consciousness center— middle mind

Imperial Heart Fire

Awareness center— lower mind

Door of Life is the true Fire under the Sea (yang within yin).

Fig. 1.8. Three minds into one

🌀 *Expand to the Six Directions*

Combining the power of the three minds into the power of the one mind, Yi, bring the Yi power into the third eye and expand it to the six directions of the universe (fig. 1.9). Connect to the universe at the crown, mid-eyebrow, heart, and tan tien.

Fig. 1.9. Expand the Yi power to the six directions of the universe.

 Create a Universal World Link

Become Aware of your Personal Star

Your personal star is an energy center located about 6 inches above the crown of your head. This star represents your higher self and connects your aural field to the universal life forces. You can become aware of your personal star by focusing on something to which you have an affinity, something with which you have some intuitive connection.

1. Make sure your tan tien is warm and that the sacrum and mid-eyebrow are breathing.
2. Be aware of the crown breathing and visualize a star or a small sun above you.
3. Be aware of the crown and feel a light beam extend out of the

crown. Make a connection to the star above you. Keep on breathing until you make a strong connection.

4. Feel how the star above you is exercising a strong pulling force on your crown. Once you can feel this pull on your crown, you will also feel a strong pull downward from the earth.

5. Be aware of the star above and of the earth and universal force below you. Feel that both of these forces, above and below, have a strong pull on you.

The way of the Tao is vast and varied, and cannot be pinned down by the monkey mind. Until you begin to think with your heart, you will not know the Tao. We will use your personal star as a focal point off which to reflect your energy down to somewhere else.

◎ Link Personal Stars, Energy Body, and Universe

1. With the Yi power, connect to your personal star 6 inches above your head (fig. 1.10).

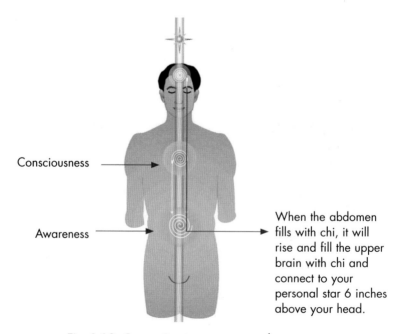

Consciousness

Awareness

When the abdomen fills with chi, it will rise and fill the upper brain with chi and connect to your personal star 6 inches above your head.

Fig. 1.10. Connecting to your personal star

2. Expand your awareness and consciousness to your personal star and out to the whole universe (fig. 1.11).

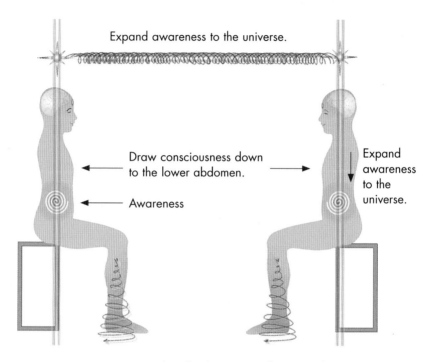

Expand awareness to the universe.

Draw consciousness down to the lower abdomen.

Awareness

Expand awareness to the universe.

Fig. 1.11. Link with other personal stars and expand the awareness from the abdomen up into the crown, then expand from the crown out to the universe.

3. If in a group, spiral the energy out and link your personal star with the personal stars of everyone in the group. Create an energy body, linking everyone together with the heart of the universe (see fig. 1.12 on page 18).
4. Link to friends, instructors, others in the Universal Tao, or others who are doing similar work around the world (see fig. 1.13 on page 18).
5. When you link to the heart of the universe (God), you attain a state of unconditional love (see fig. 1.14 on page 19).

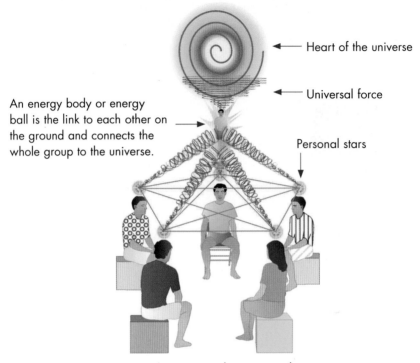

Heart of the universe

Universal force

An energy body or energy
ball is the link to each other on
the ground and connects the
whole group to the universe.

Personal stars

Fig. 1.12. A group can connect their personal stars to create an
energy body that links the whole group to the heart of the universe.

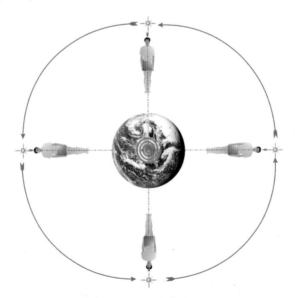

Fig 1.13. Like a satellite, the World Link meditators become a
communication link between the earth and the universe.

Fig. 1.14. Linking to the heart of the universe (God)
is being in unconditional love.

THE PROTECTIVE AND SACRED CIRCLE OF FIRE

We live in a molecular sea, and this is important to remember when engaging in any of these meditations. This particular method uses formulas to structurally place the molecules in such an order that through your thought patterns become dense, collected molecules in space, molecules that can serve as focal points for directing energy through your mind. This is accomplished by focusing on the desired result to create a field of intention. Just as a paintbrush transforms a blank canvas into a painting, this focus on a positive outcome is a creative, transformative process. Where the mind goes, the body goes. We are capable of practicing telepathy, transporting our inner intention through space and time, but we have lost the art of internal cultivation.

We have gone outside ourselves because we have lost a connection with our own divinity. Through these formulas, we hope to bring back this intention and focus to the lives of our readers.

Implicit in any spiritual practice is a need to protect your person. Whenever dealing directly with the creative potential of the universe, we always want to make sure that we are creating good, positive intentions for our work, and are guarding against negative intentions. If we are not careful as we engage in this powerful creative process, we could create or perpetuate counterproductive structures and ideas that undermine the good we produce in our practice. The Protective and Sacred Circle of Fire is a structure created to serve the function of ensuring a positive energetic presence in our practice.

Sometimes the idea of caution implies that there is something bad out there. There is nothing in the universe but that which we put into it in the form of our intentions and thoughts, good or bad. That is why it is so important that we live intentionally and with purpose. Left to our own devices, the upper mind, with its limited perspective, will take over. By nature, it finds limitations and breaks ideas down into their component parts. This is a destructive energy that when used without intention can create undesirable results, especially when what we need is to build up positive structures in ourselves and our society. "Nothing is good or bad, but thinking makes it so."

The Sacred Circle of Fire is one of many protective energy fields, and it can be used as a generator for building and storing positive energy. It has the power to protect us from all evil, whether it be sickness, misfortune, or the negative thinking of those around us (fig. 1.15). Simultaneously, it allows us to connect with the positive energy of

Fig. 1.15. The Sacred Fire Circle and Golden Chi Field have the power to protect us from evil and the negative thinking that surrounds us.

those around us and to the power of the universe. This is why understanding the intention behind the Sacred Circle is of paramount importance.

Among many things, the Circle helps us remove doubts of our own worthiness, so that we might reclaim the best that life has to offer, which is something we all have a right to share. Additionally, the Protective Ring connects us with the elemental essences of forces in the universe that both strengthen and protect us.

Using the Sacred Circle of Fire to Create the Golden Chi Field

This method is an inner visualization, using the power of the three minds (those of observation, consciousness, and awareness) fused into one mind, the Yi. Its purpose is to get in touch with the guardian essence (or guardian angel) or the forces of the six protective guardian animals of the six directions.

First, however, the Golden Chi Field must be created to protect the individual meditator and to broadcast good intentions to the whole world, which receives the energy. The Golden Chi Field is made up of the Protective Ring and the Circle of Fire.

When we use our awareness and consciousness, we turn our visualization into actualization. Using our own trust and belief, we can manifest our good intentions.

1. Visualize and imagine a big cauldron burning with fire in the cosmos (see fig. 1.16 on page 22). Feel the awareness and let it happen.
2. Now imagine that cauldron within your navel igniting your tan tien fire, kidney fire, and heart fire (see fig. 1.17 on page 22). Let the fire rise to your third eye and expand out in the six directions.
3. Be aware of yourself holding a long wand created with the power of your Yi. Reach out to the cauldron and ignite the wand with fire (see fig. 1.18 on page 22).

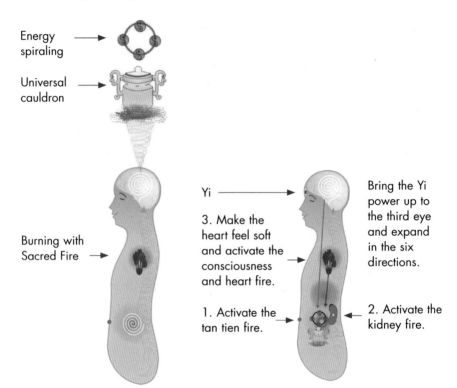

Energy spiraling

Universal cauldron

Burning with Sacred Fire

Yi

3. Make the heart feel soft and activate the consciousness and heart fire.

1. Activate the tan tien fire.

Bring the Yi power up to the third eye and expand in the six directions.

2. Activate the kidney fire.

Fig. 1.16. Project a cauldron of fire burning in the cosmos.

Fig. 1.17. Activating the Yi

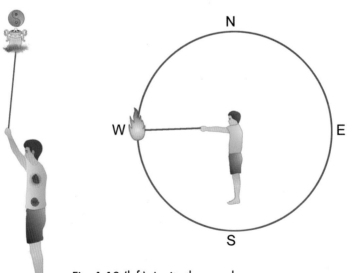

N

W

E

S

Fig. 1.18 (left). Ignite the wand.
Fig. 1.19 (above). Ignite the circle.

4. Use the Yi power to draw on the ground with the burning wand a Circle of Fire 7 feet (about 2 meters) in diameter (fig. 1.19).

5. Stand in the center facing the north with the wand pointing directly overhead. Then drop the wand in an arc until it points directly at the north (fig. 1.20). Imagine the burning wand light up the northern section outside the circle with fire. Pass the wand in an arc toward the south edge of the circle and ignite the southern section with fire. Then swing it to the eastern edge and ignite the east. Finally, swing it to the western edge of the circle and ignite the west. Light up the north. Light up the south. Light up the east. Light up the west.

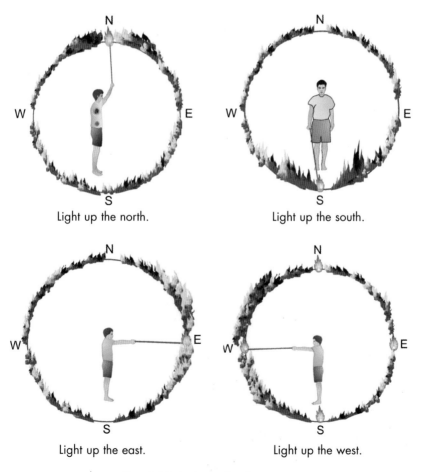

Light up the north.

Light up the south.

Light up the east.

Light up the west.

Fig. 1.20. Lighting the directions

6. Squat down in the center of the circle. In each direction, place a protective animal (guardian essence or angel): To the north place a Blue Tortoise, to the south a Red Pheasant, to the east a Green Dragon, and to the west a White Tiger. Place a Yellow Phoenix above (center), and a Black Tortoise below (earth) (fig. 1.22).

Fig. 1.22. Protective animals

Fig. 1.23. Golden Dome Chi Field

7. Create a domelike protective Golden Chi Field over you (fig. 1.23). Let go of all concerns and empty yourself. Ask each animal for protection. These Protective Animals of the six directions are the same protective animals that are associated with the vital organs. Therefore, for energetic protection, ask the Blue Tortoise for gentleness, Red Pheasant for joy, Green Dragon for kindness, White Tiger for courage, Yellow Phoenix for fairness, and Black Tortoise for stillness. Connect with universal love, saying, "I am worthy of divine love and protection."

Creating a Golden Dome as a Group

Just as one works as an individual to create a Golden Dome in order to make a field of protection and come into contact with our guardian animals, we can perform this powerful exercise as a group. When we are performing this exercise together with other like-minded people who are also filled with positive energy and good intentions, we can join our own good energy to the energy of the group to create a strong force field of protection and good will (fig. 1.24). As a group,

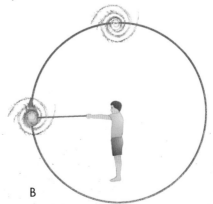

Use the Yi power to draw the Sacred Fire Circle on the ground around your house, office, and the room in which you work.

Fig. 1.24. A. Create a group energy body. B. Sacred Fire protection.

we spiral the energy out to create an energy body, linking everyone together with the heart of the universe. Working together, we call for the protection of our sacred animals and activate the eight elemental forces of nature (fig. 1.25).

Activate all eight forces of nature: wind, mountain, fire, and

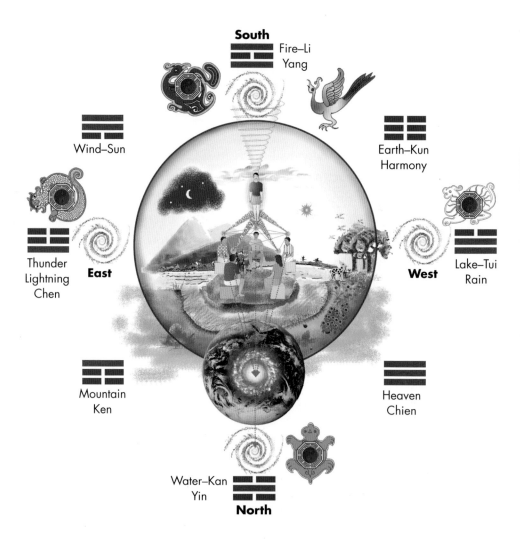

Fig. 1.25. Create and surround yourself with a chi dome
and the guardian animals.

thunder on the east; earth, lake, water, and heavenly power on the west (fig. 1.26). Call the eight forces: fire (Li), water or ocean (Kan), thunder or lightning (Chen), lake or rain (Tui), earth (Kun), mountain (Ken), wind (Sun), and heaven (Chien).

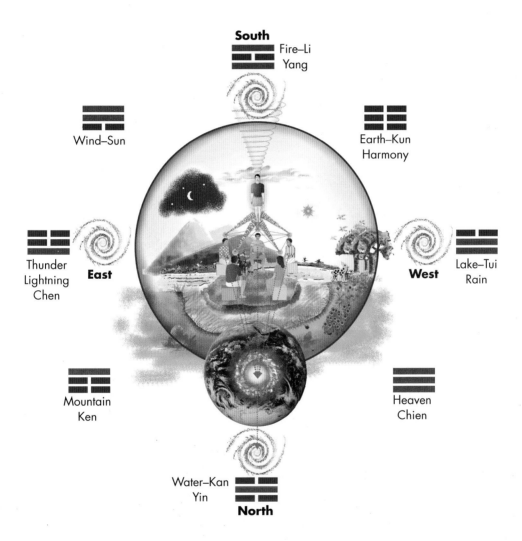

Fig. 1.26. Activate the eight elemental forces.

The World Link of Protective Healing Meditation Practice

The purpose of this meditation practice is to realign ourselves with our highest natures and then to project our best and highest energies out into the universe. To be happy with ourselves is to heal ourselves. To accept others' diverse natures of being is to accept our own experience of the world and be content. To be happy to help and heal others; to be happy to create, project, and manifest our goals; and to accomplish them in a virtuous way—this is true well-being. With these directions for healing yourself and others, you will have the tools to effectively manifest your positive desires in the world.

Aligning the Energy Field with Affirmations

The intention of affirmations is to put the energy field in focus for what you're trying to do. Like building a fire, you need to have good wood. Likewise, you have to align your thought patterns with an affirmation to gain alignment within yourself and to set the temper for your work. This creates the platform for you to get the whole engine in gear. You create an energy field to support this bigger energy field.

By manifesting this system, you create the opening for moving into a whole new gear, so to speak. You raise your vibration.

1. Empty the mind by smiling to the lower tan tien and direct the conscious mind of the heart down to the awareness of the lower tan tien.
2. Combine the three minds to fuse into the one mind (Yi) (fig. 2.1). The Yi mind is the most powerful mind to use to connect with the universe.
3. Repeat the following affirmations while touching the part of the body indicated or picturing the people indicated in your mind.

I am at peace, feeling love and compassion in myself. (Touch heart.)
I am calm, warm, and still in my center. (Touch lower abdomen.)
I am at peace with my family and people close to me. (Picture them.)
I am at peace with my neighbors. (Picture them.)

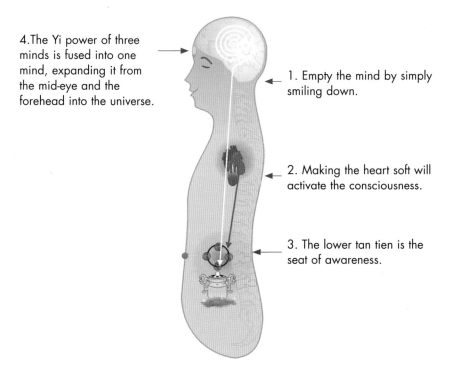

4.The Yi power of three minds is fused into one mind, expanding it from the mid-eye and the forehead into the universe.

1. Empty the mind by simply smiling down.

2. Making the heart soft will activate the consciousness.

3. The lower tan tien is the seat of awareness.

Fig. 2.1. Yi power in three minds

I am at peace with my friends and coworkers. (Picture them.)

I am at peace with my community. (Picture them.)

I am at peace with my enemies and offer them love. (Picture them.)

By repeating these affirmations you create a structure on which the creation can manifest. Just as your upper and lower minds create a structure in which your heart can live and breathe love, affirmations create a structure in which you can breathe life into your intentions. By manifesting this structure, you create the opportunity for engaging life in a whole new gear. You raise your vibration.

Healing Yourself and Others

1. Empty the mind by starting a smile in your face. Let the smiling energy flow down to the neck and into the heart area (the seat of consciousness). Make the heart feel soft and full of love, joy, and happiness, activating the conscious mind.

2. Continue smiling and relaxing down to the abdomen (the center of awareness). Smiling, empty the mind and senses (eyes, ears, nose, and mouth) down until the navel area feels warm, activating your awareness.

3. Feel the observing mind of the brain and the conscious mind of the heart going down to combine with the awareness mind of the lower tan tien. Fuse these three minds into one mind, Yi, at the mid-eyebrow. Expand the awareness out from the abdomen beyond your physical limits to the cosmos and universe, connecting with the universal energy (God).

4. Take the Yi and spiral it upward through the crown into the vast pool of energy in the universe. Continue spiraling in the universe and let it multiply. Then spiral it down to your personal star and into your whole body.

☻ *Healing with Forest Green Energy*

The beautiful light of emerald-green energy that is manifest in the universe is cleansing, pure, and transformative. Partaking of this, your body and mind are greatly nourished by its energy and strength.

1. Picture an ancient forest with bright green leaves up in the universe. Then picture a beautiful emerald green light coming from heaven and spiral it downward toward yourself (fig. 2.2).
2. Spiral the green light down through your community, your home, and then into your crown (fig. 2.3).
3. Let it clean your whole body—binding and absorbing any negativ-

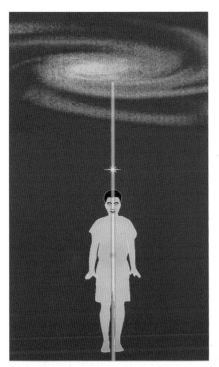

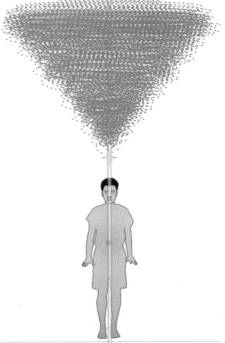

Fig. 2.2. Forest green energy: Keep the tan tien warm and expand the Yi mind to the universe, picturing a beautiful emerald green light in the universe.

Fig. 2.3. Spiral the green energy down through your community, your home, and then into your crown.

ity, burdens, worries, and sick energy to it, and draining it all out of your body (fig. 2.4).

4. Dig a hole and bury the sick, negative energy in the ground (fig. 2.5). Let the energy flow down deep into the ground. Let your heart be happy.

Repeat 3–6 times, or 36–81 times for serious illness.

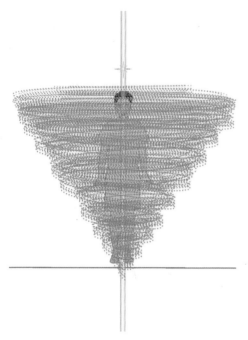

Fig. 2.4. Let the energy cleanse all that it comes in contact with.

Dig a hole and bury the sick, negative energy deep into the ground, never to return. It will be transformed by the earth into positive energy.

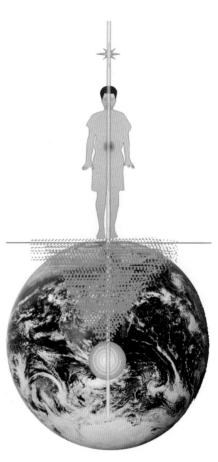

Fig. 2.5. Spiral the energy down into the ground and bury any sick energy.

⊚ *Healing with Ocean/Sky Blue Energy*

Earth energy is by nature a transformative energy. The earth absorbs pollutants, solar energy, positive and negative energies—anything connected with the earth plane will be absorbed. The earth feeds off negative energy; that is its food, which it transforms—just as the composting process transforms dead leaves into humus—into positive energy. This is all part of the creative cycle; if we eat the negative energy, we get sick and die. The earth's ability to transform negative into positive explains its resilience and longevity.

An important distinction to note is that when we pollute we are not destroying the earth; we are destroying the habitat in which humans can live. By misusing our environment, we've created a huge imbalance in the creative cycle. This stems from the thinking of the monkey mind, which sees itself as separate from the rest of creation. Taoists differ from other people on the planet in that they have a practical way to undergo transformation, but the human thinking process has to change or we're not going to be around long enough to find out what works.

Blue energy is naturally a healing energy. It is creative and life bringing to all that dwell on the earth. This energy moves and swirls in an intimate interplay between the cosmic violet energy and the deep green energy of the earth. This in-between space allows for inspiration from both the physical and spiritual realms, creating a unique orientation of the energy.

The sky has long been seen as the father (or creative energy), when compared to earth, the mother (or destroyer energy). They are two forces in a divine dance in which the sky nourishes the earth with its sunlight and rain. The sky encompasses our atmosphere and acts as a protective layer from the sun's ultraviolet energy, which in too-large quantities can burn us. At the same time, because the atmosphere allows beneficial sunlight to pass through, the sun nourishes all living beings on Earth. Certainly without the energy coming down from the sky in its various forms, there would be no life on Earth.

Mentally, this energy also represents truth, inspiration, and wisdom. If you think about it, truth often shines forth from a divine inspiration where the speaker actually puts aside his rational, thinking mind and speaks from the heart. Without the censoring, doubting, thinking mind in place, wisdom grounded in the truth of the universe is able to shine through.

1. Picture an ocean/sky blue light cooling down your body, rinsing and flushing it out like water.
2. Let a blue light spiral down, increasing in power, spiraling down through your community and your home, then into your crown and into your whole body (fig. 2.6).

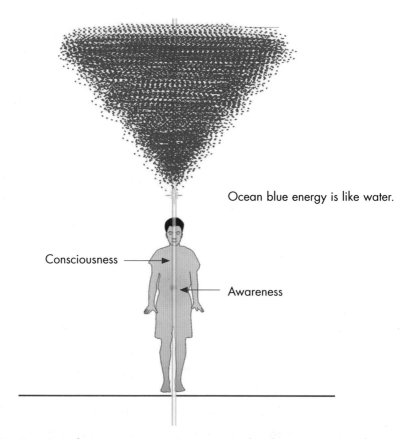

Ocean blue energy is like water.

Consciousness

Awareness

Fig. 2.6. Keep the tan tien warm. Stay connected to the awareness and consciousness of the Yi as you flush the blue light through your body.

3. Let it flush out all the remaining sickness and negativity and wash it down into the ground.

Repeat 3 times.

☯ *Healing with Universal Electric Violet Energy*

The blue-violet energy of the universe has immense inspirational power. Its energy is higher than all the other color energies and has electrochemical power. The energy has a sour flavor and stimulates the nervous system upon viewing. The blue-violet energy is connected with the third eye, which governs our intuition and stimulates our spiritual nature.

This energy has the potential to become very disconnected from physical reality. It is the energy of the stars, and thus relentlessly pulls us toward our higher nature. Striking a balance with this force and our own physical reality can prove challenging, since they are on opposite ends of the spectrum. Violet's high vibration can make some people feel uncomfortable and even ill in its presence, especially if they are not well balanced in their own energetic makeup.

However, when this energy is understood and developed appropriately, our affiliation with it can empower us to connect with all things divine, opening up a whole new world of reality of which we were not aware before.

1. Picture violet light, the most abundant energy in the universe. Picture it coming from the North Star and the Big Dipper as you fix their images 6 to 9 feet above your crown (see fig. 2.7 on page 36).
2. Gather energy in the cup of the Big Dipper, now filled with violet light, which gathers chi from the North Star and the universe. Reach up with your left hand and hold on to the handle of the Big Dipper. Pour this violet light down to your personal star 4 to 6 inches above your head. Then let it flow down to your crown.

Fig. 2.7. The North Star is a major source of violet light. The Big Dipper is a major source of red and infrared light.

3. Spiral the energy farther down and let it fill all the cells of your physical body and the energy, or soul, body.

   Repeat 6 times.

↻ Healing and Strengthening the Whole Body

1. Fill the brain with violet light, saying, "Let all sickness go away and let the brain be at its very best."
2. Follow that method for your organs, using the same affirmation for every organ. You can group the organs with the affirmations.
   • Eyes, ears, nose, mouth, tongue, and teeth.
   • Thyroid, parathyroid, thymus, pancreas, and prostate.
   • Lungs, heart, stomach, small intestines, and large intestines.
   • Liver, spleen, kidneys, uterus, and ovaries or testicles.

Doing this with your mind, stay conscious of the lower tan tien. Expand your awareness to the universe, and the universe will fill you with healing energy (fig. 2.8).

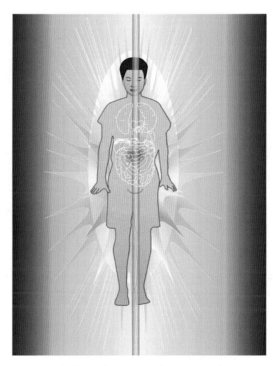

Fig. 2.8. Feel your whole body radiate
with shiny white light.

❂ Activate the Bone Marrow and the Immune System

1. Touch the sacrum and feel your fingers grow long with chi and penetrate into the sacrum and bone marrow (fig. 2.9).

2. Activate the bone marrow. Put your mind into the tan tien and the universe. Hold until the universe fills the sacrum and rises up the spine to the forehead. Feel the pulsating in the temple bones. This increases the production of healthy white blood cells for the immune system. Keep the tan tien warm and feel the chi flow up the spinal cord, then let it spiral up into the universe. The universe will fill you with healing energy.

3. Activate the immune system. Empty the mind down. Keep the tan tien warm. Touch above the pubic bone and feel your fingers grow long with chi. Let them penetrate into the sacrum and bone

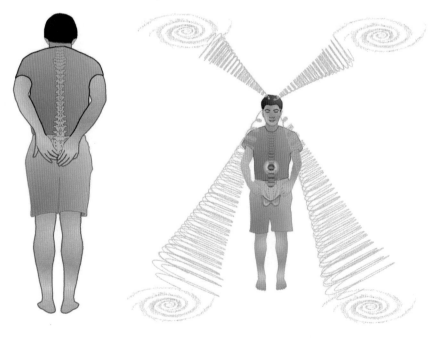

Fig. 2.9. Hold until the universe fills the sacrum and rises up the spine to the forehead.

Fig. 2.10. Touch and feel the bone. Leave your fingers there. Lower your mind into the tan tien and connect with the universe.

marrow to activate the immune system's production of red and white blood cells. Leave your fingers there and lower your mind into the tan tien and the universe (fig. 2.10). Feel the funny, happy, laughing, and tingling electrical sensations in the bones.

4. Touch the femur's middle point (upper legs) and feel your fingers grow long, penetrating the bone marrow of your legs (fig. 2.11). This should give a tingling sensation through the whole leg. It also increases the production of red blood cells.

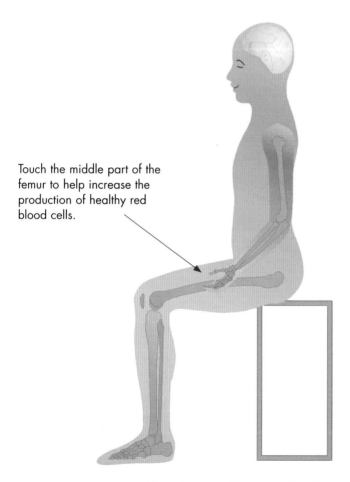

Touch the middle part of the femur to help increase the production of healthy red blood cells.

Fig. 2.11. Touch the middle point of the femur.

5. Touch the middle point of the humerus (upper arm) and feel your fingers grow long, penetrating the bone marrow of the arm, activating production of healthy red blood cells (fig. 2.12).

6. Touch the sternum, feeling your fingers grow long (fig. 2.13). Project the chi into the chest cavity, activating the thymus gland. Feel the connection to the thyroid and parathyroid glands. This activates the immune system and increases the production of T-cells (the antivirus commando cells of the body).

Fig. 2.12. Touch the middle point of the humerus.

Fig. 2.13. Touch the sternum and let the chi spread through the sternum and rib cage into the tan tien and the universe, activating the thymus gland and stimulating the production of white blood cells in the immune system.

Manifestations: Virtuous Mind Power

Overcoming Subconscious Guilt

In order to increase the Virtuous Mind Power, you need to get rid of subconscious guilt. The whole process of the Tao is about letting go. Our subconscious guilt complexes are major obstacles to our health and progress. They are the major causes of illness and frustrations. It is as if we have an inner program that says we do not deserve to have health, wealth, and happiness. This guilt makes us feel like powerless victims.

Other guilt complexes assume that we are sinners requiring punishment in the form of ill health or misfortune. We can never bring ourselves to ask the universe for anything that we do not feel worthy to receive. God made man in his own image. Humankind is naturally entitled to everything that the earth and the universe can provide for its happiness and well-being. As children of God, we deserve the best. We can command the cosmos, providing that we make our command in the right way and with good intentions.

O Reflections

What are the reasons that I cannot have _____?

What happened in the past for which I must still punish myself?

O Countering Affirmation

"I release myself from the bondage of these past events, and step confidently into a loving and powerful human existence."

Dealing with Feelings of Being Unwanted

Being unwanted is one of the worst situations in which many people find themselves. This is true for all those who feel alone, but especially for children and old people who might feel left alone to die. Subconsciously they will send out messages to the cosmos to make themselves sick, and the more attention that is given to sickness and ill health, the more energy is received from the cosmos to make that happen. We receive exactly what is projected by the subconscious mind.

O Reflections

How do I meet my needs for attention and intimacy?

How does this way of meeting my needs undercut my power and the power of others to show up as virtuous, loving presences in my life?

What new way of meeting my needs for attention and intimacy can I create that is supportive and affirming to all involved?

O Countering Affirmation

"I accept myself for the glorious being that I am. I am lovable, and have numerous sources of love and affection that fill my intimacy needs."

Overcoming Negative Self-Talk and Negative Thinking

Every thought, whether positive or negative, is a command to the universe. If our lives are not how we would like them to be, it is because we have unwittingly given negative commands to the cosmos, thereby receiving negative results. Humans have a deep need for love and attention. Sometimes we become needy and try to get sympathy and attention through being sick, helpless, or by becoming a victim. If our subconscious mind believes that our motives are unrighteous or impure, then the cosmos will keep us poor, sick, or both.

Your command to the cosmos always brings results. We get exactly what we command, whether good or bad. Therefore, we must be careful of what we think, feel, and say. If we want our lives changed for the better, we must remove all the unworthy, guilty, sinful thoughts and philosophies, and replace them with the realization that we are the children of God (the cosmos).

We must gladly accept the best that the universe and the earth have to offer. Be glad to see that other people have honestly gained wealth, health, and happiness. If we develop jealous or negative feelings toward them, then we immediately return to the state of being self-righteously poor.

We need not accept the results of our negative thinking. We can initiate a positive course of action. To fully use this power, we must replace negative thought patterns with a new command of the cosmic force. We must take action when receiving its energy and information.

O Reflections

What are my constant, negative complaints about life?

What is it that is missing?

How can I turn my negative statements about what is missing into positive statements about what is present?

O Creating Positive Energy

1. A way to get extra energy is by breathing red light into the heart 3 to 6 times. Let it radiate into the heart.
2. Spiral the energy and let it radiate throughout the whole body.
3. You will feel love energy, which will help you to take the actions necessary to complete your tasks.

❷ Making Direct Commands

To make a positive statement is to make a direct command. A command given in the present tense—in the now—is the most powerful command to the cosmos that we can give. A command to the cosmos should be phrased clearly as an individual statement and should always be said aloud.

For example, if we make the command to ourselves, "I am well, I am healthy, I am happy, I am wealthy," it doesn't matter how sick or poor we are. The fact is that we have already begun to take on that quality because of the command that we have given.

The change will begin very rapidly. The cosmic force will begin work on our inner functions immediately, according to what we have claimed we already are. Success in using cosmic power depends upon our working with and our exercise of the command in the right way to take action and responsibility. Practicing positive mind power, fusing the three minds into one, the Inner Smile, or Chi Kung will help.

Once you have set the cosmic force in motion with a direct command, you must take action. You must be willing to take responsibility for yourself. The universe cannot accomplish everything on its own. The key is to use the cosmic force to aid your actions. There is no limit to what the individual can accomplish when combining the cosmic force with individual intent.

◎ Manifest Your Positive Reality

Expand your positive statements to that which you are seeking to bring into your reality.

1. Create three powerful statements that you can recite daily.
2. Recite them daily!

◉ Manifestations of Yi Mind Power

There are actually four levels on which our manifestations come into existence: the physical, emotional, mental, and spiritual levels. Energy is constantly swirling through all of these realms, and something is always being created. What we must do as humans is intentionally participate in that process in order to produce what we want to see in our life.

There is not any one realm that is better than another when initiating the creation process, but all realms must eventually be involved to effect real, lasting transformation. Change is merely the interim process of all the levels attempting to align to a new intention, and it is merely temporary. Transformation occurs when all four realms of existence are in alignment with a new existence; thus form comes from the formless. Of course, if alignment is not reached and our focus wanes, our existence returns to what it once was before we set our energies into motion.

The universe is a mirror, and anything that you project out will bounce back with a greater magnitude. This is why it is so important to remain focused and create the thoughts we send out to the universe, rather than let our reactions rule our existence.

In the beginning, there is just consciousness, merely thoughts sent out there into empty space that come back and manifest on the physical realm. Everything you have in your life comes from your thought forms. We do it all the time; we're just not conscious of it. Anything you attained in life, you thought it out before it ever showed up.

○ Manifesting Your Affirmations

We begin to manifest our affirmations in the physical, emotional, mental, and spiritual body by first manifesting from the center of our awareness, the lower tan tien, and building up the system in order to broadcast out to the universe.

1. Place your attention in the abdomen or lower tan tien. Start with smiling and empting the mind to fuse the three minds as one (Yi) in the lower abdomen.
2. Next, bring the thought that you want to manifest up to the heart connection, then to the upper mind, the frontal lobe, and the third eye (see fig. 2.14 on page 46).
3. Create a triangle from the third eye to the temple bones, filling it with chi. The triangle creates a focal point for the energy (see fig. 2.15 on page 46).
4. Expand the awareness to the universe and broadcast the energy out to the whole universe. This affirmation is multiplied many times over by the abundance of the universal energy. It will return to you to be manifested. You must wait with your awareness anchored in the second brain of the lower abdomen.

Your center of manifestation is the frontal lobe.

Manifest the mind power using the frontal lobe. Activate by touching the sacrum. When the sacrum is filled with chi, it will rise to fill up the frontal lobe.

Sacrum

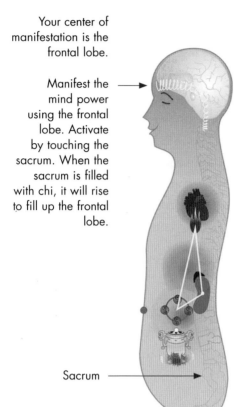

Fig. 2.14. Mind power and manifestation

Fig. 2.15. Third eye and temple bones in a triangle

O Physical Image

1. Picture yourself at the age you would like to be and hold that image very clearly (fig. 2.16).

2. Hold it in the center of your second brain (lower abdomen) and move it up to the center of your consciousness in the heart area.

3. Continue to hold this image very clearly and move it up to the mid-eyebrow on the forehead.

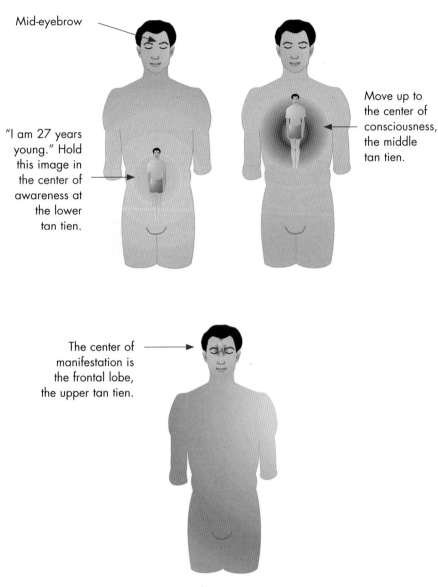

Mid-eyebrow

"I am 27 years young." Hold this image in the center of awareness at the lower tan tien.

Move up to the center of consciousness, the middle tan tien.

The center of manifestation is the frontal lobe, the upper tan tien.

Fig. 2.16. Manifesting on the physical level

4. Then send it out to the universe in all six directions (see fig. 2.17 on page 48), saying, "I am well and perfectly healthy."

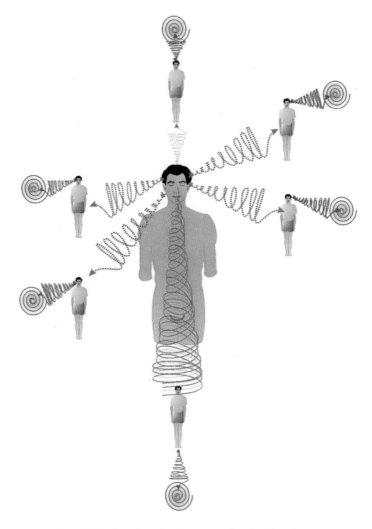

Fig. 2.17. Sending the image to the six directions

O Emotional Image

1. Picture your emotional body: See a body-shaped image close around your physical body, composed of all kinds of moving colors, saying: "I let go of old emotional experiences, seeing them for what they are, and fill myself with radiant joy, love, and compassion" (fig. 2.18).

2. Bring the image up the heart center and then to the frontal lobe.

3. Send it out to the universe, and the universe will multiply it many times. It will be sent back to you. Just wait for it to return, with your awareness in the lower brain.

O Mental Image

1. Picture your mental body, saying: "I make an agreement with myself to enjoy the best of life and to live to my full wealth potential in harmony with nature and the universe" (fig. 2.19).
2. Follow the same sequence of moving the image up to the heart, the frontal lobe, and out to the universe.
3. Wait for the return, with your awareness in the lower brain.

O Spiritual Image

Picture your spiritual body, saying: "I am at one with my God (source) within and manifest its glory."

Follow the same procedure as before.

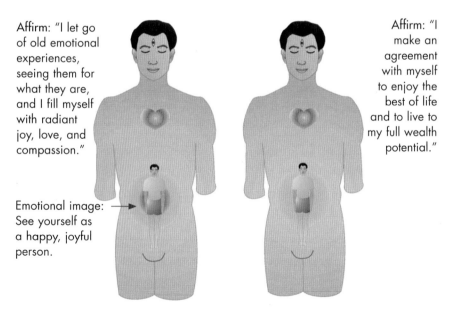

Affirm: "I let go of old emotional experiences, seeing them for what they are, and I fill myself with radiant joy, love, and compassion."

Emotional image: See yourself as a happy, joyful person.

Affirm: "I make an agreement with myself to enjoy the best of life and to live to my full wealth potential."

Fig. 2.18. Affirmations   Fig. 2.19. Affirmation of full potential

Finish the World Link of Protective Healing meditation practice by resting for a few moments and collecting the energy in your lower tan tien.

Using the World Link Meditation Process for Problem Solving

Connect to Universal Energy for Solving Problems

1. Take the questions and problems that you have into your center of awareness (abdominal brain), then to your consciousness (heart brain), and send them out into the universe through the third eye in your observation center (mind brain), broadcasting out to the whole universe.
2. Wait for the best answers and solutions to return to you clearly and distinctly. Allow them to ripen into full understanding.

Problem Solving in the Future

At any point in the future, if you have any questions or have a problem that needs to be solved, all you need to do is to inhale deeply and allow your awareness in the abdomen to expand far beyond your physical limits.

Exhale your problem into the universe, open yourself, wait for a moment, and let go of the problem. You will become conscious of the solutions to your questions or problems. The more you practice this, the more quickly and easily the results will come.

Take Action by Accessing Extra Energy

You must take action when you receive the universal energy and information.

1. The way to get extra energy is by breathing red light into the heart 3 to 6 times. Let it radiate into the heart.
2. Spiral the energy and let it radiate throughout the whole body.
3. You will feel a lot of energy, enabling you to take action and complete the task.

❧ Clarifying Your Life's Purpose

You can use the same technique to project your goals and the time frame in which you wish to accomplish them. Sometimes it helps to ask for more wisdom from the universe or cosmos in order to understand your true life's purpose.

Summary of the Complete Practice

PREPARATORY WORLD LINK PRACTICES

These practices prepare the individual or group to both project healing energy to the heart of the universe and to receive the healing energy from the universe. They also teach practitioners how to repel negative energy and ensure the creation of positive energy while doing the practice.

Centering Meditation

The centering meditation empties the mind to the lower tan tien, the seat of awareness.

Activate the Consciousness of the Three Fires in the Tan Tien, Kidneys, and Heart

1. Tan tien fire (abdomen): Feel the energy behind the navel become warm as you direct a golden-sunshine smile down from your eyes.

2. Fire under the Sea (kidney): Move the yang energy from the

adrenals on top of the kidneys down into the center of each kidney at the Door of Life, thus lighting the Fire under the Sea. Expand the energy to the Door of Life.

3. Imperial Fire (heart): Activate the consciousness by smiling down to the heart. Feel the fire of love, joy, happiness, and compassion creating softness in the heart. Make a triangle, connecting the heart to the kidneys to the lower tan tien. Connect the fireball to the kidneys and back to the heart.

4. Fuse the three minds into one mind (Yi).

5. Expand to the six directions.

Create a Universal World Link

1. Become aware of your personal star.

2. Link personal stars, energy bodies, and the heart of the universe.

Using the Protective and Sacred Circle of Fire to Create the Golden Chi Field

1. Visualize a big cauldron burning with fire in the cosmos.

2. Ignite your tan tien fire, kidney fire, and heart fire. Let the fire rise to your third eye and expand out in the six directions.

3. Hold a long wand created with the power of your Yi. Ignite the wand with fire from the cauldron.

4. Use the Yi power to draw on the ground with the burning wand a Circle of Fire 7 feet (about 2 meters) in diameter.

5. Stand in the center facing the north, then drop the wand in an arc pointing north, then south, then east, then west, igniting each arc respectively.

6. In each direction, place a protective animal: to the north (Blue Tortoise), south (Red Pheasant), east (Green Dragon), west (White Tiger), above or center (Yellow Phoenix), below or earth (Black Tortoise).

7. Create a domelike protective Golden Chi Field over you. Connect with universal love, saying: "I am worthy of divine love and protection."

8. Remain in this position for several minutes. Be aware of the Sacred Fire burning all around the circle and the Golden Chi Field surrounding you, protecting you from all evil.

THE WORLD LINK OF PROTECTIVE HEALING MEDITATION PRACTICE

The purpose of this meditation practice is to realign ourselves with our highest natures and then to project our best and highest energies out into the universe. When you master this meditation for healing yourself and others, you will have the tools to effectively manifest your positive desires in the world.

Aligning the Energy Field with Affirmations

1. Smile down to your lower tan tien and direct the conscious mind of the heart down to the awareness of the lower tan tien.

2. Fuse the three minds into one mind, Yi, at the mid-eyebrow. Expand the awareness out from the abdomen, connecting with the universal energy.

3. Repeat the affirmations listed on pages 29 and 30 while touching the part of the body indicated or picturing the people indicated in your mind.

Healing Yourself and Others

1. Take the Yi and spiral it upward through the crown. Then spiral it down to your personal star and into your whole body.

2. Healing with forest green energy: Spiral the green light down through your community, your home, and then into your crown. Repeat 3–6 times, or 36–81 times for serious illness.

3. Healing with ocean/sky blue energy: Spiral the blue light down, increasing in power, down through your community and your home, into your crown, and into your whole body. Repeat 3 times.

4. Healing with universal electric violet energy: Gather the energy from the Big Dipper and the North Star and spiral it down to fill all the cells of your body and the energy body. Repeat 6 times.

5. Healing and Strengthening the Whole Body: Fill the brain with violet light, saying, "Let all sickness go away and let the brain be at its very best." Use the same affirmation for every organ group.
   * Eyes, ears, nose, mouth, tongue, and teeth
   * Thyroid, parathyroid, thymus, pancreas, and prostate
   * Lungs, heart, stomach, small intestines, and large intestines
   * Liver, spleen, kidneys, uterus, and ovaries or testicles.

6. Activate the bone marrow: Touch the sacrum and penetrate into the sacrum to activate the bone marrow with chi. Keep the tan tien warm and feel the chi flow up the spinal cord and up into the universe.

7. Activate the immune system: Touch above the pubic bone, penetrating into the sacrum and bone marrow to activate the immune system's production of red and white blood cells. Touch the middle point of the femur and humerus to increase the production of healthy red blood cells.

8. Activate the thymus gland: Touch the sternum, projecting the chi into the chest cavity, activating the thymus gland and connecting to the thyroid and parathyroid glands, which increases the production of T cells.

Manifestations: Virtuous Mind Power

1. Overcoming subconscious guilt: We can never bring ourselves to ask the universe for anything that we do not feel worthy to receive. Overcome subconscious guilt by speaking the affirmation, "I release myself from the bondage of past events, and step

confidently into a loving and powerful human existence."

2. Dealing with Feelings of Being Unwanted: Subconsciously, those who feel unwanted will send out messages to the cosmos to make themselves sick, and the more attention that is given to sickness and ill health, the more energy is received from the cosmos to make that happen. Counter feeling of being unwanted by speaking the affirmation, "I accept myself for the glorious being that I am. I am lovable, and have numerous sources of love and affection that fill my intimacy needs."

3. Overcoming Negative Self-Talk and Negative Thinking: Every thought, whether positive or negative, is a command to the universe. If our lives are not how we would like them to be, it is because we have unwittingly given negative commands to the cosmos, thereby receiving negative results. Counter negative energy and create positive energy by breathing red light into the heart and spiraling it throughout the body.

4. Making Direct Commands: A command given in the present tense is the most powerful command to the cosmos that we can give. A command to the cosmos should be phrased clearly as an individual statement and should always be said aloud. To manifest your positive reality, create three powerful statements, such as "I am well," "I am happy," "I am wealthy," and recite them daily.

5. Manifestations of Yi Mind Power: Our manifestations come into existence on four levels: physical, emotional, mental, and spiritual.

   • *Physical Image.* Picture yourself at the age you would like to be and hold that image in the center of your second brain (lower abdomen) and move it up to the heart area. Send it out to the universe in all six directions, saying, "I am well and perfectly healthy."

   • *Emotional Image.* Picture your emotional body, saying, "I let go of old emotional experiences, seeing them for what they are, and fill myself with radiant joy, love, and compassion." Bring the image up to the heart center and then to the frontal lobe. Send it out to the universe.

- *Mental Image.* Picture your mental body, saying: "I make an agreement with myself to enjoy the best of life and to live to my full wealth potential in harmony with nature and the universe." Bring the image up to the heart center and then to the mid-eyebrow. Send it out to the universe.
- *Spiritual Image.* Picture your spiritual body, saying: "I am at one with my God (source) within and manifest its glory." Bring the image from your lower tan tien to your heart center and from there to your frontal lobe. Send it out to the universe.

Finish the meditation by resting for a few moments and collecting the energy in your lower tan tien.

USING THE WORLD LINK MEDITATION PROCESS FOR PROBLEM SOLVING

Once you have made the world link connection to universal energy you can access this energy for solving problems and answering questions that come up in your life. All you need to do is send your questions and problems through your lower tan tien and heart center and out to the universe through your third eye. Soon the best answers and solutions will return to you clearly and distinctly. As you become more adept at accessing universal energy, you can solve problems by simply inhaling deeply and allowing your awareness in the abdomen to expand far beyond your physical limits. When you exhale your problem into the universe and let go of it, you will soon become conscious of the solution. Use the same technique of exhaling your questions to the universe when seeking to clarify your true life's purpose.

You must take action when you receive the universal energy and information. Breathing red light into the heart and circulating it throughout your body will give you the energy you need to complete the task.

CONCLUSION

We entered into the experience of this mediation with the intention of healing ourselves and the world. But through this experience, we gained access to so much more. For by the time that we decide that there is something to heal, our being is already in crisis.

Every day, people walk around in various levels of health and wellness. They rarely realize how unhealthy their current mode of being is until their body reacts to some crisis it is in regarding its current state of health. Regularly practicing this meditation series allows us to constantly heal the bruises and wounds inflicted on us by our day-to-day life in this world. In this way, our aches and pains do not suddenly become major crises when the tipping point is reached.

The healing process began with understanding our own nature and seeing how we had trapped ourselves in one mode of thought, which limited our ability to express ourselves fully. We learned that the middle mind acts as a gateway for connecting the upper and lower minds.

By fusing the upper, middle, and lower tan tiens, we came to experience life more fully and connect with our true potential as humans on this earth. We now have the ability to live and understand life on a grand scale, while sacrificing very little in the process. Indeed, we have gained access to a much broader array of experiences that are deeper and more fulfilling than those accessed by living simply within the perspective of the upper mind.

By fusing the three minds, we stepped into our personal power and began to call forth, as a united front, the protective energies of the cosmos to assist us in our endeavor to expand our consciousness and live life more fully. We created the Sacred Circle of Fire for protection on this journey not from outside forces, but from our still-imperfect selves. The Sacred Circle broadcasts to the universe that no matter in what state we find ourselves, we are dedicated to creating a positive space for the potential of reaching above and beyond our current mode of living toward something higher, more glorious and more unified with the universe. The universe is inherently good, and in order to practice with it and be supported by it, we must resonate with its nature.

The fusion of the three minds brings us back to a basic level of being that is pure and unblemished by negative thought patterns. Indeed, negative patterns cannot be perpetuated when the three minds are truly fused. Creating the Sacred Circle from this space ensures that no negative energy will enter our work as we move forward with the practice.

In addition to protecting us, the Sacred Circle acts as our first gear for revving up our spiritual engine and personal power. Working in a group, everyone must rev up their engines together to create the Golden Chi Field so that they may manifest high levels of positive energy within the universe. The Golden Chi Field invokes the elemental energies around us, anthropomorphized through the protective animals we invoke, each representing an aspect of the universal energy.

With the Sacred Circle of Fire and the Golden Chi Field created, we moved into second gear and began to invoke the elemental energies that we only touched upon in the setup. We invoked the green, blue, and violet energies of the universe so that they might each contribute their unique aspects to our healing work.

First, we invoked the green transformative energy, which induces the transformation that we seek in ourselves. This green energy teaches us that in order to transform, we must first peel away the layers that have built up over the years to make space for new layers of being.

Second, we invoked the blue creative energy to replace what we gave up by invoking the green energy. The blue energy empowers us to fuse the green and violet energy into a well-balanced manifestation to benefit our world, whether that be a healthy body, mind, or spirit.

Last, we invoked the violet spiritual energy to connect ourselves with our highest levels of being and then bring that down to our material lives on this earth. This violet energy is of a high vibration, and we need to balance its presence with that of the other energies so that we can invoke it on a level that resonates with us. This happens naturally when all the energies are invoked together, mixing and whirling in a cosmic dance of balance and harmony.

At this point we began healing the body from a place of calm repose. We brought chi to every organ in the body and began to activate the immune system through its numerous channels. It is easy to activate an increased level of well-being by simply bringing attention to our immune system. It was made to respond to any need as it appeared within the body; certainly a simple request from the Yi mind power can also affect it. In this way, we began to heal ourselves on the physical level.

Then we brought our attention to the emotional level. What are some of the common emotional complexes that prevent us from being all that we truly are? Here we explored subconscious guilt, feelings of being unwanted, and negative self-talk. We also explored some tools to help reprogram our minds from those unhelpful patterns. Direct commands and affirmations to our being are designed to make very clear our intentions, especially coming from an intentionally created healing space. From there, we harnessed Yi mind power to create physical, emotional, and spiritual images that empower and uplift us toward our higher selves.

Now, having become more aware of ourselves and how we relate to our own healthy state of being, we have immense tools in our toolbox to address the constant evolution of our presence on this earth. You can trust yourself to have all the answers you need if you but look inside yourself for inspiration.

To conclude the meditation series, we always come back to the lower tan tien, storing any excess energy there, and then, finally, we rest. A rest period allows the effects of the meditation to sink in, increasing the power with which they will manifest.

What have we learned in our journey through our own body? We now know that the healing process is not simply meant to diagnose and treat, but is a dynamic, holistic process of encountering our whole being and integrating all the disparate parts more fully to achieve a higher state of balance and harmony. We wish you the very best that life has to offer.

 Appendix

Supplementary Practices

The following practices will strengthen your connection to the universal force so that you may perform the World Link of Protective Healing meditation practice from a position of optimum clarity and energy.

Activating the Six Directions and the Three Fires

This powerful energetic technique teaches you how to expand your mind and chi, to touch the force in the cosmos, and to draw that energy back into the body. By practicing the Six Directions daily you will increase your healing and cosmic power. When you achieve the Three Minds into One Mind, begin expanding into the six directions, beginning with the direction straight down below you.

Direction Below

As you do this step, trust and believe that your visualization will turn into actualization: your hands become long; your feet become long, going all the way down into the earth and out past it, into the galaxy below on the other side. Then go down through the galaxy, way beyond to the primordial force. It's as though you are extending all the way to the primordial force 30 million years ago or before (fig. A1).

1. Stand with your feet together. Put your hands down parallel to the ground. Press your hands down and smile into the ground. Expand yourself deep down into the earth—very, very deep down into the earth.
2. Push, moving the hands forward six inches only. When you push, connect with the galaxy below.
3. Pull, moving the hands back by the sides; as you pull, think about your tan tien filling with chi. Smile to your tan tien, dark, deep, and vast.
4. Push: touch the primordial force in the universe.
5. Pull back the dark primordial force with your hands to your tan tien. Push and pull: project your awareness into the vast empty space. Then come back to your tan tien, which is also empty, just like the primordial condition before anything existed, the source of all. Push and pull 3 to 9 times.

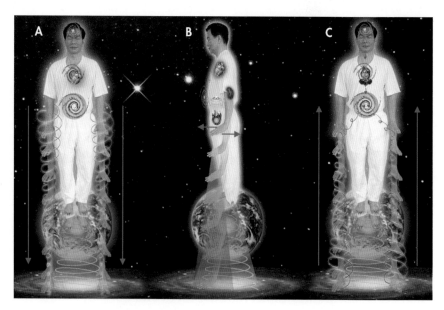

Fig. A1. A. Hands expand through the earth and to the galaxy below.
B. Hands push forward and pull back. C. Smile to the primordial chi
from the universe as it is drawn in to fill the tan tien with chi.

⚙ *Front Direction and Tan Tien Fire*

Next, be aware of the front direction; a huge fireball appears in front of you. Open your palms: scoop up the chi; scoop up the fire. Bring the fire into your tan tien. Activate the tan tien fire (fig. A2).

1. Start with a small dot of light inside you. Expand your awareness, smiling to the universe in front of you.
2. Become aware of a big fireball in front of you. Feel your hands becoming bigger and longer. Scoop up the fireball. You may close your eyes to help your inner senses.
3. Use the fireball to light the fire in your lower tan tien. Feel the fire burning in the darkness, the "fire burning under the sea."

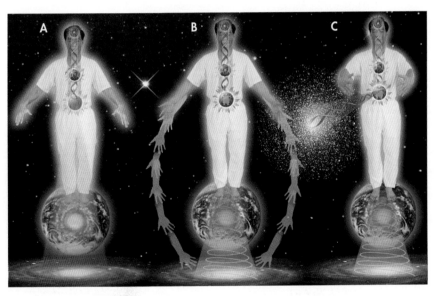

Fig. A2. A. Be aware of the universe in front. B. Expand your hands very big and long to the universe in front. C. Hold the fireball to activate the lower tan tien fire.

◌ Back Direction and Kidney Fire

Be aware of the back of the tan tien, the Door of Life, and the back or rear direction. Extend your mind very far away to the back. Scoop up the fire and light up your "kidney fire" (fig. A3).

1. Expand your awareness all the way to the back. Move the arms toward the universe behind you.
2. Touch the universe; scoop up the fire. Activate the kidney fire. Maintain your awareness in the tan tien and expand, smiling out to the universe. The energetic spiral glows in the tan tien. Spiral in the heart, spiral in your crown, and spiral in the universe.

Fig. A3. Be aware of the back direction, move the arms toward the universe behind you, and scoop up the universal fire.

◌ Heart Fire

Raise your hands under your armpits, and feel yourself holding two fireballs. Touch the heart by extending the fingers energetically in from the sides; feel your hands extending into your heart and very far away. Activate the heart fire (fig. A4).

1. Move your hands under your armpits and extend your fingers deep into your heart. Keep your awareness on the infinite space to the sides.
2. Connect to the tan tien and increase the fire in yourself.
3. Feel your heart soft in the center of the chest as you smile down. Feel the warmth of the fire, and the energy of love, joy, and happiness in the heart.
4. Feel the connection with the unconditional love in the universe as you keep your heart consciousness in your tan tien and extend your awareness out to the universe.

Fig. A4. Activate the heart fire.

❷ *Sacred Fire (Chi Fire, Holy Fire)*

Connect the three fires to combine into one fire: heart to kidneys to navel to heart (fig. A5).

1. Move your hands together in front of your heart.
2. Connect the heart fire to the kidney fire, the kidney fire to the tan tien fire, and then back up to your heart.
3. Connect them all as one triangular sacred fire, circulating the chi among the three centers, first slowly, then getting faster and faster.

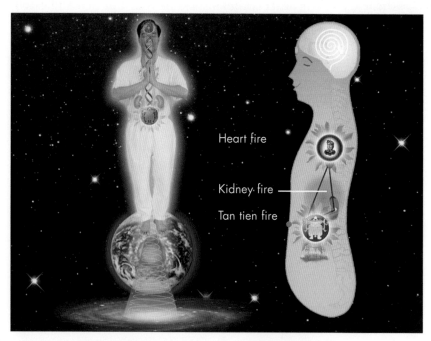

Heart fire

Kidney fire

Tan tien fire

Fig. A5. Connect the three fires and the sacred fire.

❷ Opening the Third Eye to the Six Directions

Now extend your hands out to the front, very far away—pushing, pushing, pushing. Turn your palms inward, and extend your middle fingers inward toward your third eye. Picture a crack in the middle of your forehead, and pull the crack open. Feel the light from the heavens opening it and feel the light from the heavens shining into your brain.

1. Open your palms. Open your eyes. Look to the universe. Extend your hands to the front, palms vertical. Extend the arms from the scapulae. Smile and touch the universe (fig. A6).

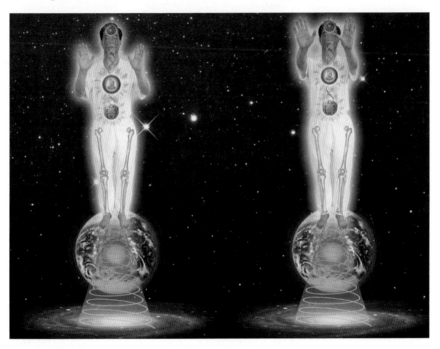

Fig. A6. Look out as you smile into the universe in front of you.

2. Turn your palms inward and extend your middle fingers inward toward your third eye.
3. Picture a crack in the middle of your forehead and let the heavenly light shine into the brain; pull the crack open and let the light reflect into the organs (see fig. A7 on page 68).
4. Close the third eye. Pull: open, close, open, close. With the third eye open, the light from the heavens shines into your brain and reflects down to all your organs. Open and close the third eye 3 to 9 times.

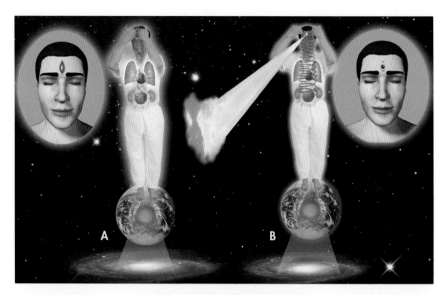

Fig. A7. A. The middle finger hooks into the third eye and light reflects down into the organs. B. Pull open the third eye; let heaven open and shine its light into the brain.

🌀 Front Direction: Push/Pull Master Practice

This is the master practice that is imperative for successful completion. When you first start practicing you should do it at least 100 times and increase up to 200 times. Push and pull. When you push, feel your hands extend far away—very long—and reach into the sky. Touch the universe. Turn the visualization into the actualization.

1. Push: Extend your arms and hands to the front, palms vertical. Extend the arms from the scapulae. Expand: smiling, touching the universe—touching the force, touching the cosmic chi (fig. A8).
2. Pull: Draw the chi back to you from the universe. Moving the arms from the scapulae, draw the hands toward your body in a horizontal position, drawing the chi into the lower tan tien (fig. A9).

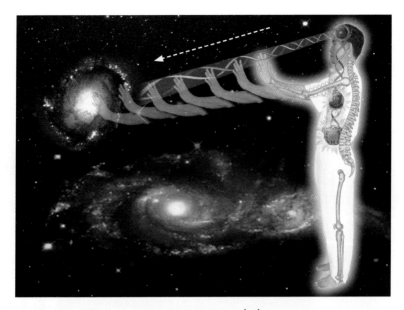

Fig. A8. Master practice: touch the universe.

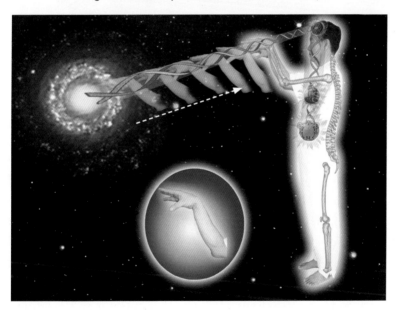

Fig. A9. Drawing in universal chi—feel your tan tien and fill it with chi.

3. Push, very far away to the universe. Pull. Push, smile, relax, and let go, touching the sky, touching the universe (see fig. A10 on page 70).

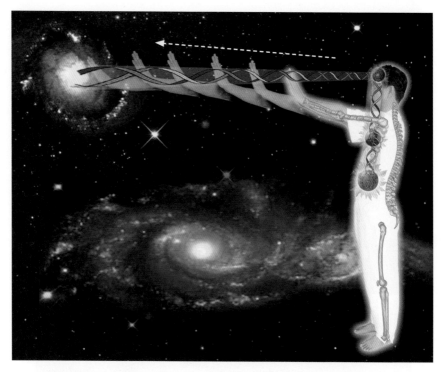

Fig. A10. Let go—push and touch the universe 6, 9, or 18 times.

◑ Left and Right Directions

Now move your hands to the left and right directions. Pull the universal energy in. Push; touch the universe. Pull; think about your tan tien. Push, all the way, touching the universe.

1. Move your extended hands from the front horizon to the left and right sides and push to touch the universe (fig. A11).
2. Pull into the tan tien: Smile to your tan tien. Keep smiling to your tan tien (fig. A12).
3. Push to both sides. Expand all the way, smiling and touching the universe.
4. Push and pull, touching, reaching into the universe, drawing in the chi. Smile energy into you from both sides (see fig. A13 on page 72). Do this 3 to 6 times.

Fig. A11. Touch the universe—left and right.

Fig. A12. Pull: just feel your tan tien.

Fig. A13. Draw the chi in from both sides.

⊘ Direction Above

1. Turn your palms up to the universe and fill the bones of your hands and arms with chi (fig. A14).
2. Scoop up the chi. Pour the chi over your crown, and touch your crown. Project the chi all the way down to the perineum and down through the earth to the universe below (fig. A15). Connecting your tan tien and the universe, always feel your tan tien, heart, and crown spiraling, and the universe around you spiraling.
3. Remember to use the mind. Extend it down to the earth and gather the energy. Again extend it up to the universe and gather more energy. Bring it back down to the mid-eyebrow and bring in more energy. Gather the energy and bring it to the tan tien (fig. A16).
4. Touch the navel and feel the chi start to spiral faster and faster in the lower tan tien. Keep moving the energy. When we move it to

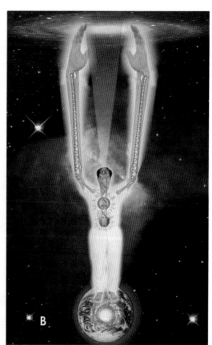

Fig. A14. A. Raise your hands to the universe. B. Feel that the hands are big and long and that the bones are hollow. Fill and pack the bones with chi.

Fig. A15. Scoop up the universal chi and pour it over the head.

Fig. A16. Gather the energy.

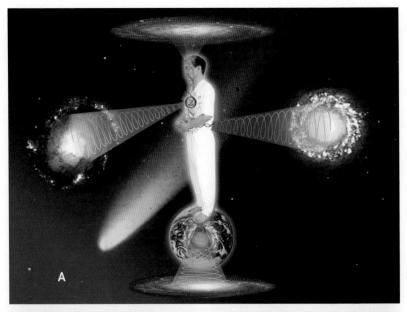

Fig. A17. A. Touch the navel and feel the chi start to spiral faster and
faster in the lower tan tien. B. Feel the tan tien and the universe
all spiraling at a fast speed.

a certain level, it gets faster and faster (spiral speed). Feel the tan
tien and the universe all spiraling at a fast speed (fig. A17).

The Cosmic Orbit Meditation

Connect with the North Star to Receive the Violet Light

1. Begin by raising the hands to the universe; feel that the hands are big and long and that the bones are hollow. Fill and pack the bones with chi (fig. A18).
2. Be aware of the North Star and Big Dipper (fig. A19).

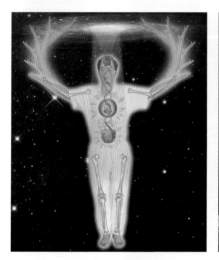

Fig. A18. Raise your hands up to the universe.

Fig. A19. Connect with the universal violet light from the North Star and Big Dipper.

3. Let the North Star and Big Dipper descend down to your hands. Use the left hand to hold the handle of the Big Dipper and pour the violet light from the universe down to your crown; then let it flow through the whole body (see fig. A20 on page 76).
4. Guide this healing light down into your skull, deep into your brain, cervical vertebrae, sternum, thoracic vertebrae, lumbar vertebrae, and down through your legs. Feel it penetrating and enlivening your bones, deep into the bone marrow: washing, cleansing, energizing (see fig. A21 on page 76).

Fig. A20. Pour the violet light down and through your body.

Fig. A21. Let your whole body feel clean and radiant,
shining with the healing light.

5. Feel this liquidlike chi spill all the way down to your feet. Feel it
connecting with the earth through the soles of your feet; be aware
of the Bubbling Springs breathing and pulsating in the feet (the
K1 point of the Kidney meridian).

❂ Open the Back-Crown Point

1. Touch the back-crown point. Pour the chi all over your crown.
2. Think of your soles so that you feel as if there is a waterfall of chi flowing from your crown all the way down to your soles.
3. Feel your fingers grow long and the chi penetrate down through your spine to the coccyx. Leave the fingers touching the back of the crown, to maintain the energetic connection with the coccyx (fig. A22).

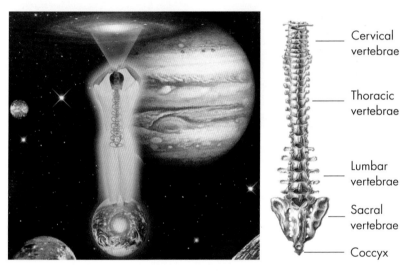

_____ Cervical vertebrae

_____ Thoracic vertebrae

_____ Lumbar vertebrae

_____ Sacral vertebrae

_____ Coccyx

Fig. A22. Feel your fingers growing long, all the way down to the coccyx.

4. Be aware of the tan tien and spiral it like universal energy in motion. Feel the heart center spiraling and the crown spiraling. Be aware of the universe spiraling above, below, front, back, left, and right, charging the three tan tiens (see fig. A23 on page 78).
5. Let all of the sick energy and the negative forces leave the body and go down into the ground for Mother Earth to recycle. Extend the chi from above all the way down through the earth and the universe below.

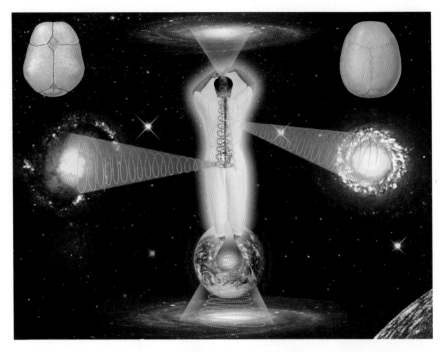

Fig. A23. Feel the universe spiraling and charging the three tan tiens.

☯ Open the Mid-Crown Point

1. Move to the mid-crown point. Touch the point and project your fingers deep through the middle of your body, down to the perineum.
2. Focus on the perineum. Feel the chi from the universe flow right to your perineum.
3. Look for one dot of light. Look into the darkness, the immense, vast darkness. This is the primordial force.
4. Be aware of the tan tien and spiral it like the galaxy. Feel the heart center spiraling and the crown spiraling. Be aware of the universe spiraling above, below, front, back, left, and right.
5. Let all of the sick energy and the negative forces go out of the body and down into the ground for Mother Earth to recycle. Extend the chi from above all the way down through the earth to the universe below (fig. A24).

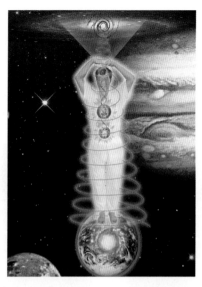

Fig. A24. Open the mid-crown point and extend the chi
from above to the earth and universe below.

❂ Open the Other Head Points

1. Scoop the energy and then come down and touch the mid-eyebrow,
   focusing on the base of the skull; feel the fingers penetrate straight
   through to the base of the skull (fig. A25).

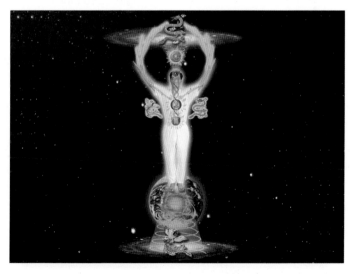

Fig. A25. Mid-eyebrow point

2. Be aware of the tan tien and the universe spiraling. With the spiraling, the chi will become hot in the fingers. It will expand and penetrate out through the back of the head all the way to the universe behind (fig. A26).

3. Move the fingers down to touch the upper lips. Feel the chi charge the upper palate (fig. A27).

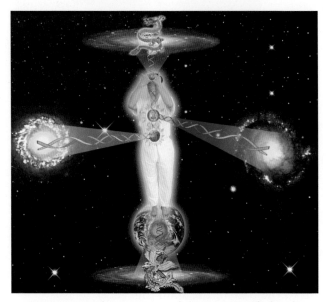

Fig. A26. As the tan tien and universe spiral, the chi penetrates out through the back of the head.

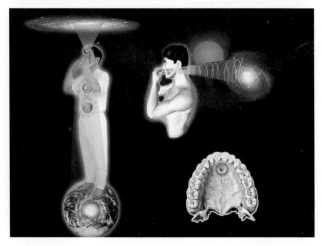

Fig. A27. Feel the chi charge the upper palate.

4. Come down to the middle of the upper lip. This point revives consciousness. Feel the universe and galaxies spiral and charge the palate. The circuits are flowing down through the tongue and to the throat (fig. A28).

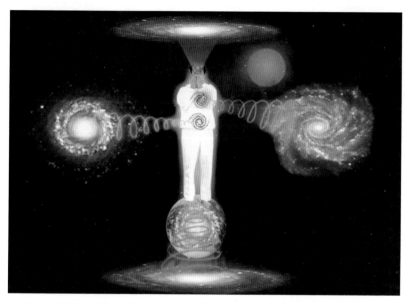

Fig. A28. Feel the universe and galaxies spiral and charge the palate.

5. Picture your fingers like laser beams of chi. Feel your tan tien and the universe spiral and charge your fingers.

6. Move your fingers out from the mid-eyebrow around the side of the head, to the top of the ears. Touch the left and right ear and feel the fingers grow very long.

7. Your laser fingers should cut open your skull in the middle, around to the top of the ear. Make a cross into the brain and open the upper tan tien, the back of the head, and the third eye to open the whole brain so chi can go into it (see fig. A29 on page 82).

8. Leave your fingers there. Spiral your lower tan tien and the universe. Concentrate on your lower tan tien spiraling your heart and crown; chi penetrates into your brain. The universe is also spiraling in all directions: above, below, in front, behind, left, and right.

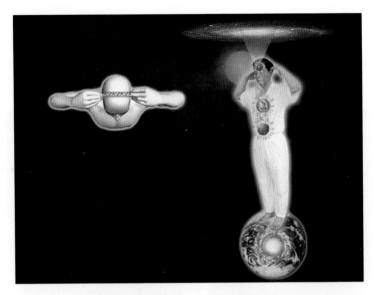

Fig. A29. Opening the Jade Pillow

Gather the chi in your lower tan tien. It is a big empty space: you can put so much chi inside there!

9. Move your hands all the way to the back, cutting to the back of the skull. Touch, and feel the upper tan tien open (fig. A30).

Fig. A30. Touch the back of your skull and feel the upper tan tien open.

10. Touch the base of your skull. Focus on the mid-eyebrow. Feel the chi flow like a laser beam from back to front and out to the universe in front (see fig. A31).

Fig. A31. Feel the chi flow like a laser beam from the back out to the universe in front.

11. Complete the opening process by moving the hands back around to the mid-eyebrow, cutting as you go.

12. Touch the upper lips and feel the connection with the tongue and the front palate (fig. A32). When you are aware of the universe spiraling, you are charging energy into yourself.

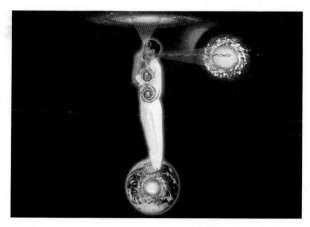

Fig. A32. Charging the upper lips, tongue, and front palate with energy

13. Move down to the throat center and touch and focus on the C7 point on the back of the neck (fig. A33). Focusing on the back of the neck and the throat center will activate the thyroid and para-thyroid and thymus glands.

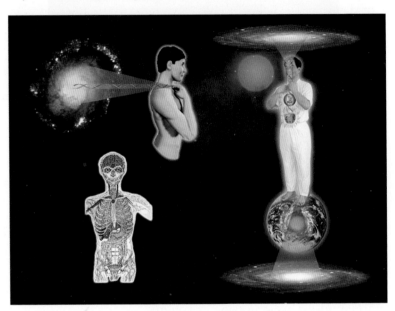

Fig. A33. Move the fingers down to the throat center and feel them penetrate through C7 and to the universe behind.

❂ Recharging Energy While Doing the Cosmic Orbit

Any time you want to recharge the energy (when you feel the hands getting low in energy and to help you open the body), reach into the universe and bring down the energy. Whenever you are scooping up the universal chi, your hands and legs will feel very warm. With your consciousness turned in and your awareness out, you are recharging your energy from the constant love and orgasmic energy all around you—the creative energy of the universe.

The inner alchemy of sexual energy takes place in the three tan tiens where yin and yang energy are merged together. In the Taoist formulas the Phoenix and Dragon symbolize the female and male. In the three tan tiens you can constantly feel male and female, Phoenix and Dragon, uniting to become one energy. This primordial love and orgasmic energy within is the most important energy that you need every day. If you want more energy, just become aware of six directions of the universe: below, above, left, right, front, and back. Everything is spiraling and moving around you. When you are aware of the universe spiraling, you are charging energy into yourself.

1. Feel that your bones and your arms and legs are hollow. Fill and compact them with chi (fig. A34).

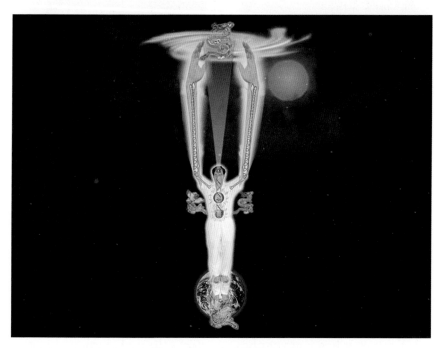

Fig. A34. Recharge your energy from the universe.

2. Scoop the universal chi and pour it down over your crown and all the way down, down, down to the middle tan tien.
3. Feel the Dragon and the Phoenix making love in the heart center. Feel the yin and yang, male and female, Dragon and Phoenix reunite, make love, spiral into one love and orgasmic force in the

heart center, lower tan tien, and the crown, and spread out to all the cells in the body (fig. A35).

Fig. A35. Feel the universal love and orgasmic energy
spread throughout the body.

🜂 Opening the Middle Tan Tien and Heart Point

1. Recharge from the universe; pour chi over the crown down through the body, and lower your hands down to the heart center. Touch with the fingertips (fig. A36).
2. With your hands at your heart center at the mid-sternum, imagine the fingers long; reach through and focus on the point opposite the heart, T5/T6 on the spine. Chi and golden light will penetrate into your thymus gland. Feel the chi penetrate through your heart all the way through T5/T6 to the galaxy behind (fig. A37).
3. In the middle tan tien and the universe also feel your fingers penetrate into the bones and bone marrow and spread out into your rib cage.

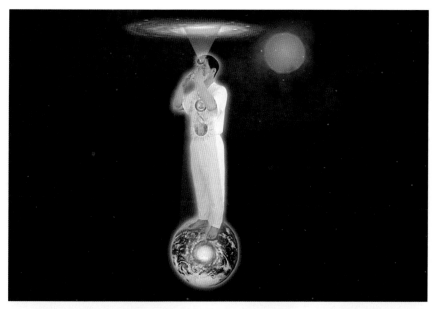

Fig. A36. Pour chi over the crown down through the body, and lower your hands to the heart center.

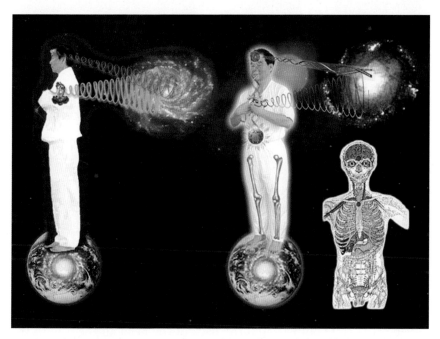

Fig. A37. Opening the heart point: touch the heart and focus on the back of the heart. Feel the energy go all the way through to connect with the galaxy.

4. Move to the left and right, opening the heart center (like opening a book), which also activates the thymus gland and all of the lymphatic system, the immune system, the T cells, B cells, and the killer cells. Opening the heart center will immensely help the immune system (fig. A38).

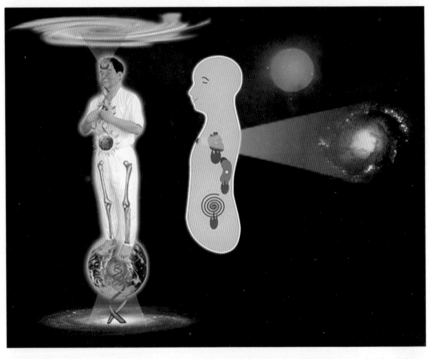

Fig. A38. The heart center is also connected to the thymus gland, which is the most important organ in the immune system.

5. To open the left and right sides of the heart, move your hands around under your armpits, extending the chi like laser beams cutting open the middle tan tien. Pause under the armpits as you send the chi into the center (fig. A39).

6. Be aware of the tan tien and the universe spiraling. With the spiraling, the chi will become hot in the fingers. It will expand and penetrate out through the back of the head all the way to the universe behind (fig. A40).

Fig. A39. Opening the left and right sides of the heart

Fig. A40. Sending heart chi out to the universe

Fig. A41. Open the back, touch the back at T5/T6,
and feel the energy come to the front.

7. Continue to move your hands around to your back at T5/T6; touch, and send the chi from back to front (fig. A.41). Let the beam of chi penetrate out through the heart center to the universe in front of you.

8. Then move the hands back to the front, cutting as you go.

❂ Opening the Solar Plexus Point

1. Move down now to the solar plexus, found between the sternum and navel (fig. A42). Touch the solar plexus on the point opposite T11 and focus on T11 on the spine. Feel your fingers penetrate all the way through.

   Think that a sun is shining in your solar plexus and radiating light throughout the whole body. Just keep on holding and feel the sun in the body. The more you can feel and see the sun shining in the body, the more you can clear the sickness from the

Fig. A42. Touch the solar plexus on the point opposite T11.

body. Sickness doesn't like light and warmth; it likes darkness and dampness.

2. Feel your chi fingers penetrate into the bone and bone marrow and spread out into your rib cage (see fig. A43).

Fig. A43. Feel your chi fingers penetrate into the bone and bone marrow.

◎ Opening the Navel Point

1. Raise your hands and charge with the chi in the universe. Feel your hands to be very big, very long. The bones are hollow and compacted with compressed universal chi.
2. Scoop the chi from above and guide it down. Pour all the way down, down, down, down to the navel.
3. Touch the navel, and focus on the Door of Life (Ming Men) opposite, on the spine between L3 and L4. Touch and feel the chi penetrate to the Door of Life. Feel the chi penetrate through to the back and out to the universe behind (fig. A44).

Fig. A44. Feel the chi penetrate the Door of Life.

4. Feel as if there is a laser beam cutting open the left and right sides (fig. A45). Begin at the navel and slowly circle all the way back to the Door of Life; all the while the energy is cutting like a laser and opening this area.

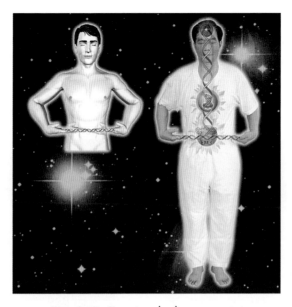

Fig. A45. Opening the lower tan tien

5. Open the lower tan tien the same way as the upper and middle tan tiens. Feel your tan tien and universe spiraling—charge more chi into your hands, and let them be like lasers cutting open your lower tan tien (fig. A46).

Fig. A46. Tan tien and universe spiraling

6. Cut around to the sides; pause. The fingers of the left and right hand are very long, extended energetically inside. Cut and feel the energy penetrate into the center.

7. Wherever you touch, focus on the opposite point and feel the energy flow (fig. A47).

Fig. A47. Tan tien and universe feel more chi.

8. Continue cutting to the Door of Life. As you touch the Door of Life, you will feel the energy go right through to the navel and into the universe (fig. A48).

Fig. A48. Touch and send the chi from the Door of Life back to the navel and out to the universe in front.

❂ Opening the Sexual Palace

Finally, move the hands back to the navel and go down to the pubic bone and focus on the back. Penetrate right through the sexual organs (ovaries/prostate and bladder area).

1. Move the hands back to the navel, extending the fingers and "cutting" the tan tien open as you go. Touch the navel; tan tien and the universe are spiraling. Feel more chi, and feel the tan tien open (see fig. A49 on page 96).
2. Touch the sexual center and let the chi penetrate through to the sacrum (see fig. A50 on page 96).
3. Touch the sacrum and let the chi penetrate through to the sexual center.

Fig. A49. Opening the tan tien at the navel

Fig. A50. Chi penetrates from the sexual center through to the sacrum.

Opening the Bones and Sacrum

When we are young, our bones produce many blood cells. The older we get, the more hollow the bones become and they slowly diminish their production of blood cells. We lose a very big factory. In the Taoist practice we work to revive this factory. Smile to your bones; feel chi going into the bones and activating the bone marrow. When you have nothing to do, just touch your bones and smile and feel funny, happy, laughing bones.

The sacrum controls all the bones and bone marrow production. Sometimes when I need to enhance my immune system I touch my sacrum and the sternum. Both of these bones are very important and help to activate the immune system and increase the white and red blood cells.

1. Begin by touching the hipbones and laugh inside the bones (fig. A51). Laugh inwardly and feel the laughing vibration in the bones.

Fig. A51. Touch both sides of the hipbones. Feel your fingers penetrate into your bones.

Feel your fingers are very long and penetrating right into your bones and bone marrow.

2. Touch the femur; feel the tan tiens and universe spiral (fig. A52). Charge the fingers. Feel the funny, happy, laughing vibration inside the bones and in the bone marrow.

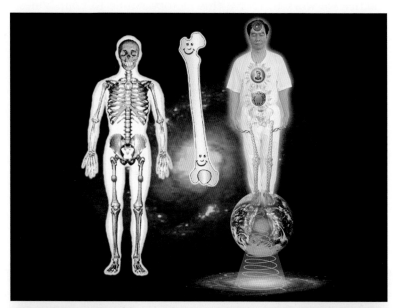

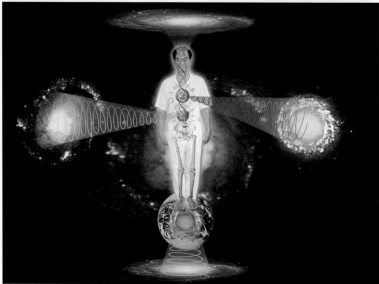

Fig. A52. Touch the femur; feel the tan tiens and the universe spiral.

3. Touch the sternum and laugh internally, sending the vibration into the bones: funny, happy, laughing bones. The marrow and thymus will activate—this is very important. Taoists describe the inner laughing as the sensation of hitting a drum and feeling the inner vibration—BOOMMMM! This is the echo of the energy vibrating in the bones.

4. Now slowly lower the chi down through the bones to the earth. Move the hands down the legs as you bend down (fig. A53).

Fig. A53. Lower the chi down through the bones to the earth.

5. Lower yourself all the way down to the ground and sit on your feet. Feel the entire body sink down into the ground and gather the earth energy. Move the chi with your hands down to your toes, down through the earth and to the universe below (see fig. A54 on page 100).

6. Touch your heels and feel the energy go up into the heel. Raise your sacrum (straighten your legs) while keeping your hands at your toes (see fig. A55 on page 100). Feel the whole area open, smile to the tan tien, and wiggle the tailbone side to side. This will open a lot of energy in this area.

Fig. A54. Squat down and move the chi with your hands down through the earth to the universe below.

Fig. A55. Raise your sacrum, keeping your hands at the toes. Smile to your tan tien.

7. Squat down again. Send the chi down to the earth and the galaxy below (fig. A56).

8. Touch your heels and feel your bones as you slowly begin to rise (fig. A57).

Fig. A56. Send chi down to the earth and the galaxy below.

Fig. A57. Touch your heels and feel your bones as you begin to rise up.

9. Raise your sacrum again, maintaining hand contact with your feet. Fill your bones with chi as you guide it up with your hands (fig. A58). Smile to your tan tien.

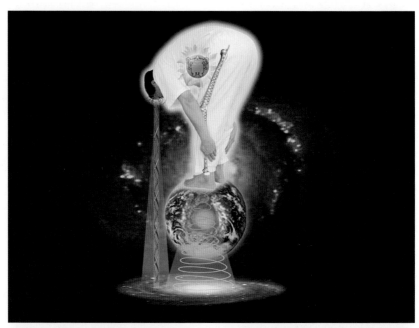

Fig. A58. Fill the bones with chi as you move your hands up.

10. For the third time, lower down. Open your palms, gathering the chi from the earth below. Gather and scoop up the chi.
11. Now reverse. When you touch your coccyx, think about the ground. The energy will go into the bone and spinal cord and reach up to the crown (fig. A59).

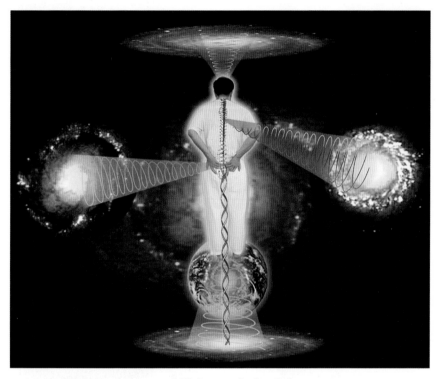

Fig. A59. Feel your bones, and fill them with chi all the way up to your coccyx. Touch your coccyx; feel the tan tiens and the universe spiraling.

❂ Opening the Governing Channel

1. Touch the sacrum and picture the sacrum growing. Make it bigger and bigger, extending it down to the universe (see fig. A60 on page 104).
2. Feel the eight holes of the sacrum breathing. The sacrum breathes the energy up into the spine (see fig. A61 on page 104).

Fig. A60. Touch your sacrum.

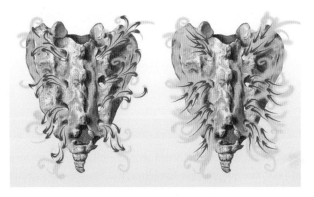

Fig. A61. Eight holes breathing

3. Feel the sacrum big and breathing. As always, when you need energy, become aware of the universe and the tan tien (fig. A62). Feel the chi rise through the spine and spread out to the glands and organs and fill them with chi.
4. Now bring your hands up to the Door of Life (Ming Men) and send energy through to the navel (fig. A63).

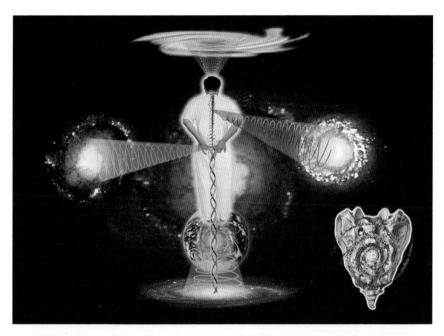

Fig. A62. Come up to the sacrum; remember the tan tien and the universe.

Fig. A63. Send energy from the Door of Life through to the navel.

5. Connect with the energy of the tan tien and the universe (fig. A64).

6. Move up to C7, opposite the throat center; feel the fingers penetrate through to the throat center (fig. A65).

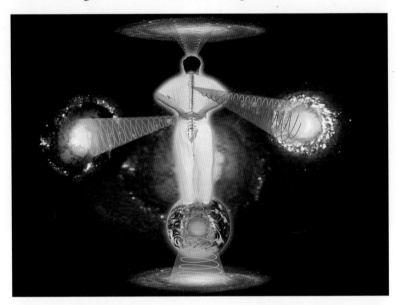

Fig. A64. Connect to the tan tien and the universe.

Fig. A65. Touch C7; feel the fingers penetrate through to the throat.

7. Fingers continue to touch the C7 point; feel the three tan tiens and the universe spiraling (fig. A66).

Fig. A66. Feel the three tan tiens and the universe spiraling.

8. Move up to the base of the skull (Jade Pillow), which is opposite the mid-eyebrow.
9. Finally, go up to the crown. Feel the energy penetrate from the crown all the way down to the perineum. This can take awhile. All you have to do is think that your fingers are *long*. It's simple. You practice it, and you have it! It's your aura that is extending and penetrating deep within your body all the way to the middle of the perineum (see fig. A67 on page 108).
10. Gather the energy and bring it back down to the tan tien. Just use the mind. Extend it down to the earth and gather the energy. Go back up and extend up and gather more energy from the universe. Come back down to the mid-eyebrow and bring more energy into the mid-eyebrow (see fig. A68 on page 108).

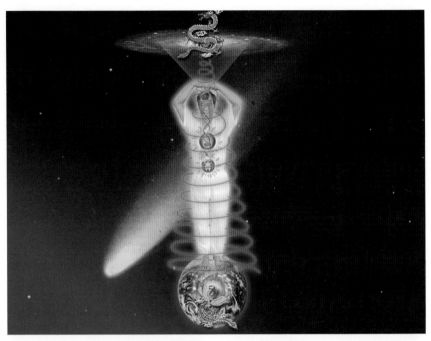

Fig. A67. Move the fingers to touch the crown and feel them penetrate through the body down to the perineum.

Fig. A68. Gather the energy.

11. Keep on moving the energy through the orbit. Touch the navel and feel the chi sink down to the lower tan tien and start to spiral faster and faster (fig. A69).

Fig. A69. Feel the chi sink down to the
lower tan tien and start to spiral.

12. In the beginning, when you move the energy slowly through the orbit, you will become aware of the spinal cord and all of the nervous system connected to the internal organs (see fig. A70 on page 110).

13. Feel the tan tien and the universe spiral faster and faster (see fig. A71 on page 110). The spiraling is at a rate of 30,000–60,000 miles per hour. When you move so fast, you become very still, just as the earth is spiraling and spinning so fast yet it feels still.

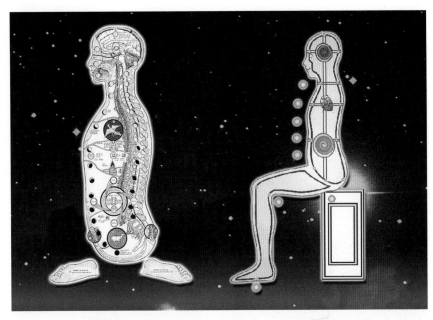

Fig. A70. Become aware of the spinal cord and all of the nervous system connected to the internal organs.

Fig. A71. Feel the tan tien and the universe all spiraling at a fast speed.

14. Sit down and start to move the energy through the orbit at a very fast speed, from 1,000 rotations per minute to 10,000 per minute, and up to 30,000 per minute (fig. A72).

Fig. A72. Sit down and start to move the energy through the orbit very fast.

When you open the orbit and the energy starts to move through it, the body will be penetrated by more and more energy. That will make the body less dense. When the body is too dense, chi and light cannot go through it. That's when sickness can start to get into the body. Doing this meditation you will get a lot of energy right through the body (fig. A73).

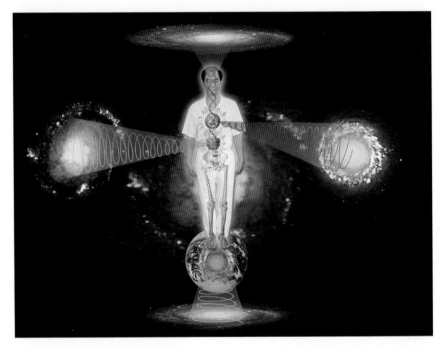

Fig. A73. Open the Cosmic Orbit and your body becomes less dense.

About the Author

Mantak Chia has been studying the Taoist approach to life since childhood. His mastery of this ancient knowledge, enhanced by his study of other disciplines, has resulted in the development of the Universal Tao System, which is now being taught throughout the world.

Mantak Chia was born in Thailand to Chinese parents in 1944. When he was six years old, he learned from Buddhist monks how to sit and "still the mind." While in grammar school he learned traditional Thai boxing, and soon went on to acquire considerable skill in Aikido, Yoga, and Tai Chi. His studies of the Taoist way of life began in earnest when he was a student in Hong Kong, ultimately leading to his mastery of a wide variety of esoteric disciplines, with the guidance of several masters, including Master I Yun, Master Meugi, Master Cheng Yao Lun, and Master Pan Yu. To better understand the mechanisms behind healing energy, he also studied Western anatomy and medical sciences.

Master Chia has taught his system of healing and energizing practices to tens of thousands of students and trained more than two thousand instructors and practitioners throughout the world. He has established centers for Taoist study and training in many countries around the globe. In June of 1990, he was honored by the International Congress of Chinese Medicine and Qi Gong (Chi Kung), which named him the Qi Gong Master of the Year.

The Universal Tao System and Training Center

THE UNIVERSAL TAO SYSTEM

The ultimate goal of Taoist practice is to transcend physical boundaries through the development of the soul and the spirit within the human. That is also the guiding principle behind the Universal Tao, a practical system of self-development that enables individuals to complete the harmonious evolution of their physical, mental, and spiritual bodies. Through a series of ancient Chinese meditative and internal energy exercises, the practitioner learns to increase physical energy, release tension, improve health, practice self-defense, and gain the ability to heal him- or herself and others. In the process of creating a solid foundation of health and well-being in the physical body, the practitioner also creates the basis for developing his or her spiritual potential by learning to tap into the natural energies of the sun, moon, earth, stars, and other environmental forces.

The Universal Tao practices are derived from ancient techniques rooted in the processes of nature. They have been gathered and integrated into a coherent, accessible system for well-being that works directly with the life force, or chi, that flows through the meridian system of the body.

Master Chia has spent years developing and perfecting techniques for teaching these traditional practices to students around the world through ongoing classes, workshops, private instruction, and healing sessions, as well as books and video and audio products. Further information can be obtained at www.universal-tao.com.

THE UNIVERSAL TAO TRAINING CENTER

The Tao Garden Resort and Training Center in northern Thailand is the home of Master Chia and serves as the worldwide headquarters for Universal Tao activities. This integrated wellness, holistic health, and training center is situated on eighty acres surrounded by the beautiful Himalayan foothills near the historic walled city of Chiang Mai. The serene setting includes flower and herb gardens ideal for meditation, open-air pavilions for practicing Chi Kung, and a health and fitness spa.

The center offers classes year round, as well as summer and winter retreats. It can accommodate two hundred students, and group leasing can be arranged. For information worldwide on courses, books, products, and other resources, see below.

RESOURCES

Universal Healing Tao Center
274 Moo 7, Luang Nua, Doi Saket, Chiang Mai, 50220 Thailand
Tel: (66)(53) 495-596 Fax: (66)(53) 495-852
E-mail: universaltao@universal-tao.com
Web site: www.universal-tao.com

For information on retreats and the health spa, contact:
Tao Garden Health Spa & Resort
E-mail: info@tao-garden.com, taogarden@hotmail.com
Web site: www.tao-garden.com

Good Chi • Good Heart • Good Intention

# Index

Page numbers in *italics* refer to illustrations.

BOOKS OF RELATED INTEREST

Healing Love through the Tao
Cultivating Female Sexual Energy
by Mantak Chia

Chi Self-Massage
The Taoist Way of Rejuvenation
by Mantak Chia

The Alchemy of Sexual Energy
Connecting to the Universe from Within
by Mantak Chia

Iron Shirt Chi Kung
by Mantak Chia

Living in the Tao
The Effortless Path of Self-Discovery
by Mantak Chia and William U. Wei

The Art of Cosmic Vision
Practices for Improving Your Eyesight
by Mantak Chia and Robert T. Lewanski

Healing Light of the Tao
Foundational Practices to Awaken Chi Energy
by Mantak Chia

The Six Healing Sounds
Taoist Techniques for Balancing Chi
by Mantak Chia

INNER TRADITIONS • BEAR & COMPANY
P.O. Box 388
Rochester, VT 05767
1-800-246-8648
www.InnerTraditions.com

Or contact your local bookseller